OPOLIS.

The Spital fields

y Gouernr orwuders B.

Pastern Gate

THE TOWRE

Beere howse

S tiliards

Tower Crane

Wolster Gate

S Mary ouerie

Towlee

Beere howse

Cum Priuilegio.

STILLIARDS) Hansa, Gothica dictio, conuentum, vel congregationem sonans, multarum ciuitatum est confoederata Societas, tum ob præsita Regibus, ac Ducib. beneficia: tum, ob securam terrà mariquè, mercaturæ tractationem, tum denique, ad tranquillam Rerumpub. pacem, & ad modestam adolescentum institutionem conseruandam, instituta: plurimor. Regum, ac Principum, maximè Angliæ, Galliæ, Daniæ, ac Magnæ Moscouiæ, nec non Flandriæ, ac Brabantiæ Ducum priuilegijs, ac immunitatib. ornata fuit. Habet ea quatuor Emporia, Cuntores quidam vocant, in quib. ciuitatum negotiatores residẽt. suosque mercatus exercent. Hor. alterium hic Londini, domestica oeconomia nitet, habens domum Gildehallã Teutonicã quã vulgo Stillard dicunt.

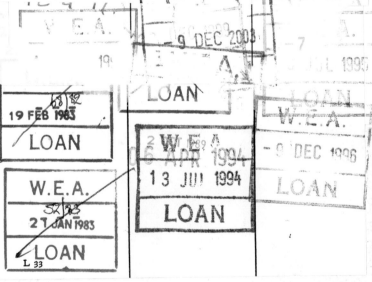

*John Stow's monument in the church of
St Andrew Undershaft* (John Freeman)

ELIZABETHAN LONDON

Martin Holmes

CASSELL · LONDON

CASSELL & COMPANY LTD
35 Red Lion Square, London WC1
Melbourne, Sydney, Toronto
Johannesburg, Auckland

© Martin Holmes 1969
First published 1969

S.B.N. 304 93322 X

B6913898

Phototypeset and printed by BAS Printers Limited, Wallop, Hampshire
F.169

TO R. E. M. WHEELER
who first set me to lecture on this subject
and consequently to make some study of it

Contents

Illustrations

With the exception of the frontispiece and Figs. 6 and 21, all illustrations are British Crown Copyright.

Preface

The reader who desires to investigate the subject of Elizabethan London at first hand is recommended to study the edition of Stow's *Annals* edited and augmented by Edmund Howes and brought out in 1632, particularly the passages describing the early years of the reign of James I, in which Howes notes a number of the principal inventions and innovations of the preceding reign. Ben Jonson, in several of his comedies, and Thomas Dekker, in *The Gull's Horn-book*, describe and satirize a number of the less desirable London types, and anonymous comedies such as *The London Prodigal* and *The Puritan* (both popularly but quite unjustifiably accredited to Shakespeare) illustrate some of the average citizen's characteristics without attacking them so savagely as do the professed satirists. The French phrase-books of Claude Hollyband and Peter Erondell, transcribed and edited by Miss M. St Clare Byrne under the title *The Elizabethan Home*, give a charming and illuminating picture of the Elizabethan small boy in relation to his parents, his teacher and his schoolfellows, while for scholarly commentary on the subject in general, Kingsford's edition of Stow's *Survey*, and the appropriate chapters of the Oxford Press compendium known as *Shakespeare's England*, are so well known that it is almost superfluous to recommend them here.

Modern biographies of Elizabeth herself, such as Elizabeth Jenkins's *Elizabeth the Great*, and the earlier *Queen Elizabeth* of Sir John Neale, are expressive studies of the central figure, and illustrate her impact on her contemporaries at home and abroad; and there is much useful and entertaining material to be gained from nineteenth-century works like the long-popular *Life* by Agnes Strickland—though some of its assertions need revising or modifying in the light of more recent research—and the collection of extracts edited by W. B. Rye under the title *England as Seen by Foreigners in the Time of Elizabeth*. For the last years of the reign, Dr G. B. Harrison's *Elizabethan Journal* is an ingenious collation of extracts from carefully-documented Elizabethan sources, covering the various matters likely to have been of the greatest general interest, be they social, political, literary or vaguely scandalous, and consequently giving a vivid picture of Elizabethan society and its table-talk; and the corresponding *Jacobean Journal* shows how manners and customs changed with the advent of a new century and a new dynasty.

It would seem that the clearest picture of Elizabethan London is to be obtained from the Elizabethans themselves. Camden's *Annals*, the earliest detailed biography of the Queen, dealing with events up to the year of the Armada, was written originally in Latin, but was translated into English by Abraham Darcie and published in 1625. Sir Robert Carey's memoirs were edited and published anonymously by Sir Walter Scott, with Naunton's *Fragmenta Regalia*, a series of character-studies of the most famous figures of the Court. Holinshed's *Chronicle* includes a long and valuable description of the Queen's progress through London towards her coronation, and the various arches, tableaux and congratulatory verses through which the city displayed its loyalty. Here, as so often in the pages of Stow, we realize that we are reading an account written by, and for, men who actually saw the events described. To all these, and to other books and friends too numerous to mention, I should like to record my indebtedness, and at the same time to thank the authorities of the various public collections who have allowed me to reproduce photographs of material in their possession.

Martin Holmes

Appleby, 1968

CHAPTER ONE

Bird's-Eye View

For our knowledge of Elizabethan London we are able to refer to two valuable contemporary sources of information, such as no earlier period can provide. At the beginning of the Queen's reign appeared the first detailed and reasonably accurate map of the Metropolis, and the closing years of the century saw the publication of the famous *Survey* written by the historian and antiquary, John Stow (*frontispiece*). For the first time in its history we are able to consider the city as a whole, from the viewpoint of the men who saw it, drew it, lived in it and described it, and our own reconstructions, based on the fragments of material that still remain, can be compared to some extent with these contemporary records.

The map is a picture-map, giving something of the effect of an air-photograph or a bird's-eye view, and in its best-known form it appears as a double-page plate in that famous Continental atlas, the *Civitates Orbis Terrarum* of Braun and Hogenberg, first published at Cologne in 1572. The London that it depicts (*Fig. 1*) is primarily the irregular semicircle, approximately a square mile in area, that lies within the perimeter of the Roman and medieval wall; but the map is of particular value in that it also covers a wider field and shows not merely the street-plan of the city, but its relation to the surrounding countryside, the neighbouring city of Westminster and the suburb of Southwark on the other side of the Thames. Its western boundary lies a little beyond Charing Cross, but not far enough to include St James's, while to the east it shows the Tower and the beginning of the untidy development beyond. North and south it naturally includes a good deal of open country, and the street-plan is therefore on a smaller scale than would have been necessary had the map been devoted to the City of London alone.

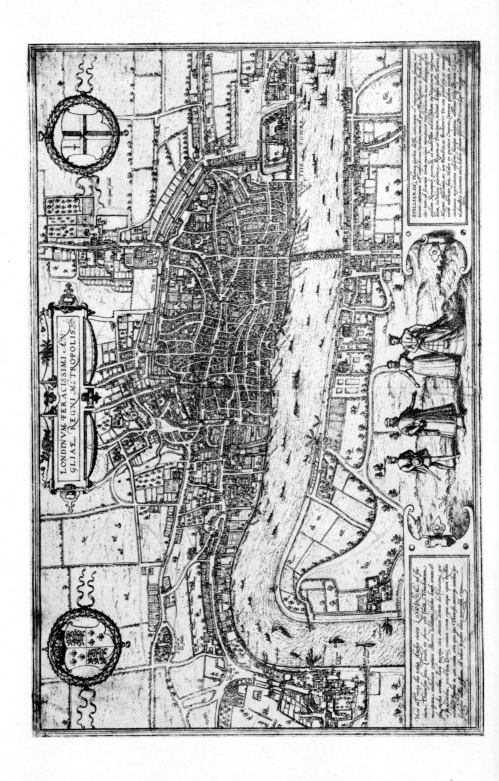

Fig. 1 *Map of London : from the Civitates Orbis Terrarum of Braun and Hogenberg, 1575. In this edition the Royal Exchange appears, the plate having been altered for its insertion after the original publication in 1572* (London Museum)

Fig. 2 *Street-plan of modern London, from Westminster to the Tower* (Ordnance Survey Sheet TQ 38 SW, reproduced by permission of the Controller of H.M. Stationery Office. Crown Copyright reserved)

Braun and Hogenberg, however, were trying to produce something fuller and more informative than a collection of city-maps, and this plate fulfils the object of the *Civitates* volume by illustrating London in its surroundings, and presenting, one might say, a portrait of the city rather than a diagram.

Fig. 3 *A group of citizens : detail from the* Civitates *map* (London Museum)

Like most of the other maps and views in that work, it includes a group of characteristic inhabitants in their ordinary costume, and this group (*Fig. 3*) tells us at first sight something important about the Elizabethan Londoner: namely that he was not a courtier but a merchant. The calf-length gown of the older man is open in front, being put on like a coat, but it is held in at the waist by a sash or narrow girdle, and by cords and buttons across the breast and on the upper part of each hanging sleeve. It is edged and lined with fur, and bands of fur frame the two openings in the sleeve, through either of which the forearm may be thrust at will. The original cuff is sewn up, and forms the bottom of a sleeve-pocket, as in more than one form of present-day academic gown. This furred garment, the small, round hat of the wearer, and the similar hat, short cassock and sword-and-buckler equipment (reversed by the engraver) of the young man behind him, all betoken the well-to-do tradesman and his senior apprentice or journeyman, attending him while he 'walks abroad'. His lady, likewise, is no elaborate court figure. Her plain stuff gown is worn open, over a bell-shaped 'Spanish farthingale', a petticoat borne out by rings of bent cane or osier-rods, but it shows no extravagance of outline; the bodice, with its two vertical 'slashes', is cut and buttoned to fit without a wrinkle, probably over a corset stiffened with whalebone or metal, and the only sign of exaggeration is to be seen in the long outer sleeves, which hang nearly to the hem of the gown behind and, for the sake of convenience, are caught together with a loop of material. The young woman in attendance would seem to be wearing no farthingale, but a plain petticoat, under her gown, the front of which is almost hidden by her apron. Her skirt is a little shorter than that of her mistress, allowing greater quickness of movement, and the back-flap of the black 'French hood', caught up and brought forward after the fashion of the time, can just be seen in the middle of her forehead.

These are the people whom we must consider as Elizabethan Londoners, and whom Franciscus Hogenberg wished his readers to consider as such when he engraved the plate. The Tudor Court had no habitual residence in London itself. The Tower, it is true, was officially a palace as well as a fortress, and Elizabeth went straight there on her arrival in London from Hatfield at the time of her accession, but it had neither the associations nor the amenities to commend it as a centre for the Court, and after this brief compliance with tradition the new Queen went up-river to Somerset House and ultimately to Whitehall. Court society in this country was still a form of elaborate country-house society, as it had been in the Middle Ages, periodically shifting from one to another of the great royal estates as the appropriate seasons went by. 'Londoners know no king but their Mayor' had been the proud contention of the London merchants of an earlier day, and at this time it was still flat cap and furred gown, not short Spanish cloak and cartwheel ruff, that betokened the Londoner of quality.

Above these pictures of Londoners, Hogenberg has engraved a picture of their city. Though on a very small scale—the whole double-page measures only some fifteen inches by twenty—it has incorporated in it a surprising amount of detail, and detail which other evidence has established as being accurate. Particularly notice-able are the nearness of London to the open country, and the paramount importance of the Thames. Gardens, orchards and pasture-land are to be seen all round the city, in some places coming right up to its protecting wall. The churches of St Giles and St Martin are seen among the fields that are now commemorated only in their names, and St Martin's Lane, running northwards into the open country, is a lane indeed. Down to the south-west, round the bend of the river, lies the independent city of Westminster, and between the two lie fields and open country again, with a long line of great houses following the river-bank and fronting on a road that still bears its riverside name of the Strand.

They were not town mansions. When they were built, they were country houses, near London but still outside it, and nearer still to Lambeth, a point that had been more important to their owners. For these were the palaces of the great provincial bishops who, when summoned to play their part in matters of government, came up from their distant sees, in full state as Princes of the Church, and established their households as near as possible to the official head-quarters of the Archbishop of Canterbury. By the time of Elizabeth's accession, the Reformation had robbed the great prelates of their splendour, their palaces along the Strand had become the houses of wealthy laymen, and Lambeth alone retained, as it still retains, its ancient function. Hogenberg's Lambeth Palace is simply, almost crudely, rendered, and measures rather less than an inch across, but it is still recognizable as the Lambeth Palace of today, and the modern visitor can see that impressive gateway not very much altered from the form in which it appeared when the first Elizabeth was young.

The street-plan, by its very congestion and near-confusion, suggests the busy, bustling life that went on within the compass of the walls. In a way, London's commercial success had contributed to her discomfort. The roads and lanes had been laid down in days when the city was less populous, less active and not yet the great centre of commerce that it was to become, and there had been room, in the Middle Ages, for all the traffic that they were required to carry. Horsemen in single file, pedestrians walking close to the wall and keeping clear of the drainage-gutter in the middle of the street, porters with bundles in barrows or on their backs, and strings of pack-animals with their drivers walking beside them, were not then so numerous as to cause a hindrance to one another, or to the progress of business in general. On either side of the narrow streets rose tall, wooden-framed houses, cramped in appearance but often containing wealth indoors, and every luxury but those of space and privacy. Shops, warehouses, counting-houses and the like supported larger rooms above-stairs, extending storey by storey over the roadway and furnished with varying degrees of richness. The medieval London merchant was a man who generally kept a good proportion of his property visible and available at hand, in the form of gold and silver plate. Vessels of precious metal were unlikely to depreciate in value while the price by weight remained constant; they were negotiable securities among honest men, but less negotiable, by virtue of their nature and fashion, among dishonest ones. Through the latter part of the Middle Ages, and the development of the Renaissance in England, these Londoners increased their wealth and their enterprise, and the traffic began to be still busier in the streets.

But here that same wealth and the increasing importance of the city became a hindrance. The rapid commercial development of London had increased the value of London houses to a degree that made impossible any general scheme for the revision or widening of the roadway. Any increase in the width of a thoroughfare would have involved the sacrifice of house-property on one side of it, if not on both, and most of that house-property was far too valuable to go. A London house, with the ground it stood on, constituted an important commercial asset, negotiable in time of really urgent need, but more usually held as a source of income. Shares in it, or in its rents, would form a special currency of their own. Few or none were likely to support any move to destroy a square foot of anything so valuable, or to turn it into something possibly convenient but eternally unproductive, like an extra width of roadway. It was better to put up with the inconvenience and congestion, and let the streets of Elizabethan London retain the narrowness of the Middle Ages. Some of them, for that very reason, retain it to this day.

Turning again to the map, we notice, by contrast to this tangle of narrow streets, lanes and alleys, that there is one broad, swift thoroughfare, leading from the western boundary of the city to the Tower on its eastern border, and that this is the surface of the Thames. Small boats—the famous Thames wherries—lie moored at every stair-foot, others are in active use carrying passengers up- or down-stream, slightly larger craft are moving about the upper reaches, some with sails, some with oars and one, apparently, with both, and in mid-stream, just off Paul's Wharf and the long-destroyed river-front of Baynard's Castle, is a more important vessel still. It is a tilt-boat (*Fig. 4*), a barge with a long tunnel-like canopy

7

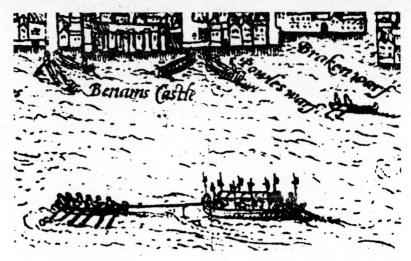

Fig. 4 *The Royal Barge on the Thames: detail from the* Civitates *map*
(London Museum)

running for most of its length, and it has neither sail nor oars, but is
towed by another boat carrying six oars a side. The main barge is
steered with a long sweep instead of a rudder, and around the central
canopy can be seen tiny figures of men with unmistakable halberds
standing up like a ring-fence. It is this detail that establishes beyond
doubt the nature of the craft. There was only one person in Elizabethan London who would travel thus, surrounded by a guard of
halberdiers and towed by a crew of liveried watermen, and that
person was Elizabeth herself. Small as the scale is, the engraver has
been able to depict for us the Royal Barge of England going up-
river to Westminster with the young Queen on board, surrounded
by her Gentlemen Pensioners, a body still in existence as the
Honourable Corps of Gentlemen-at-Arms.

For she was the young Queen still, when Hogenberg engraved the
first version of his map of London. Though the bird's-eye view we
are considering was first published, as has been said, in 1572, it
contains details that had disappeared ten or twelve years earlier,
such as the tall and slender steeple that crowned the central tower of
old St Paul's Cathedral till it was struck by lightning in 1561 and
burned down to the stonework. In addition, there have come to
light, within the last few years, two copper plates engraved by
Hogenberg's hand and used in their time for printing part of a much
larger map of London, hitherto unknown, which contains details
that are known to have been in existence at Elizabeth's accession,
but to have been removed very soon after. One of the plates is in
private possession; the other (*Fig. 5*) is in the London Museum. No

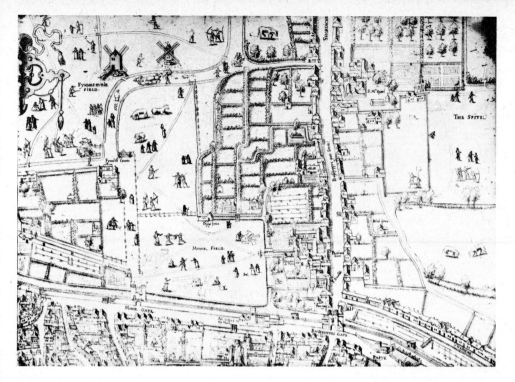

Fig. 5 *Moorfields in about 1560 : reversed from an engraved copper plate in the London Museum* (London Museum)

Fig. 6 *Diagram relating the above to the modern street-plan* (Derek Hayler)

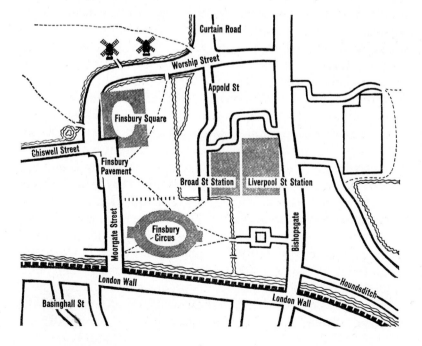

impressions from them are known, and none can be taken directly, for the fine engraving is worn so shallow with time, and with frequent service in the press, that many of the lines will no longer retain the ink. The plates must have been worn out towards the end of the sixteenth century, and have been sold or given away as scrap metal, because each one has come into the hands of a painter and been made the ground of a picture. This was the practice of some Flemish artists of the time, who believed that their work gained richness and luminosity by being painted on a surface of burnished metal. The London Museum example bears a fine representation of the Tower of Babel, by Martin van Valckenborgh, its other side being engraved with a picture-map of Moorfields from Finsbury windmills to London Wall. The privately-owned plate depicts the area immediately south of this, showing a large section of the eastern side of the City, down to the riverside.

The whole map would appear to have consisted of as many as twenty plates, and something of its general appearance may be judged from a large though crude woodcut picture-map, at one time ascribed on rather inadequate evidence to the Elizabethan surveyor, Ralph Agas. It appears, however, from the Register of the Stationers' Company that in 1562 a map of London was entered for publication by Gyles Godet or Godhed, and as Godet was known as a purveyor of woodcuts, there is more likelihood that this is the map in question, particularly as it contains distortions of which a fastidiously accurate surveyor, such as Agas is known to have been, would hardly allow himself to be guilty. Only three impressions are known—one in the Guildhall Library, one in the Public Record Office and one in the Pepysian Library at Magdalene College, Cambridge—and they are all of early seventeenth-century date. The arms of Elizabeth have given place to those of the Stuarts, the letterpress in the descriptive lines at the bottom has been altered to correspond, but the map as a whole serves to give us some suggestion of the scale on which Hogenberg's great work must originally have been carried out. Two plates of detail from that lost original, one miniature version of the whole on a single plate of the same size, and a cruder, woodcut version adapted to conform to the ideas of another generation—all these can be combined to give us a coherent impression of the London to which Elizabeth came, after long months of doubt and endurance, to be acclaimed as Queen.

Her accession was greeted enthusiastically as a national blessing. It meant the end of danger and uncertainty for many, and for herself above all. Though her standing as next heir to the throne had been indisputable, there had been no guarantee that she would ever live to claim it. Bishop Gardiner of Winchester had publicly urged the desirability of her execution; there had been attempts to implicate her in the abortive rising of Sir Thomas Wyatt and his fellow-supporters of her cousin, the Lady Jane Grey, who for little more than a week had been called Queen of England, had passed from the throne to captivity in the Tower and thence, while still in her teens, to the scaffold and the block; and there were voices ready enough to advise the ailing, unhappy Mary Tudor to send her half-sister the way Jane Grey had gone. Yet for all this, Mary would not be persuaded. There was little affection between the sisters, but they were both the daughters of Henry VIII and shared certain instincts and reactions in common—witness the text of Mary's speech of encouragement to the Londoners when Wyatt was marching on their city, a speech which in its feeling, courage and actual turn of phrase rings out like Elizabeth at her best—and at times the Queen would send presents of jewellery to the younger woman who, until a child should be born to Mary and Philip, was heiress to the Crown. Nonetheless, there was no sense of security for anyone. At any moment there might be a change of mood: a turn of conscience that could call on Mary to make an end of her heretic sister in the interests of England and of the Faith that she was trying to restore; or, quite simply, an outburst of that terrible Tudor rage which could destroy an adversary and arrogantly brave the consequences. Courtiers and politicians had made tentative suit to the Lady Elizabeth in her retirement—so nearly captivity—at Hatfield House, but the Lady Elizabeth had made no sign, said no word, taken no step that could be reported as treason to the sick woman at St James's or to the Spanish king-consort who stayed abroad in Brussels, waiting for her to die. Rumours and counter-rumours were active enough with tales of Mary's death, possibly guesswork, possibly wishful thinking, possibly deliberate falsehoods intended to tempt Elizabeth to premature action and destruction, but she disregarded them all; till at last, one day in November, they brought her King Philip's betrothal ring from the dead hand of her sister, and she knew that she was Queen indeed.

Even before she herself knew it, she had been proclaimed Queen in Parliament, and thereafter, with all due ceremony of heralds and trumpeters, first in Westminster Hall and then at Cheapside Cross, the accepted centre and gathering-place of her City of London, as if that city were a separate, independent kingdom. In a sense, indeed, it was. There had been London merchants, and London officials, and a London system of self-government and self-administration, before the seven kingdoms of the Saxons had been forged into the one kingdom of England; and through the centuries the original market-town, set at the point where road and river met, had developed into a great port and commercial centre, by far the largest and richest in the country. Westminster was the royal city, centred on the shrine of a saint and the palace of a king; but London was itself, a proud medieval *commune* that had earned the right to be recognized and respected for the unique institution it had become.

At the very outset of the new reign we see the tangled street-plan of London exercising its influence. Elizabeth's route from her semi-imprisonment at Hatfield House would lead her straight to Aldersgate, and she might therefore have been expected to enter her capital by that gateway, but she stayed some days at the Charterhouse (a former priory, but by that time the dwelling of Lord North), then struck eastwards along the Barbican and made her official entry at Cripplegate. Study of the early maps will quickly show the reason. The other gate was set in an angle of the wall, the streets immediately within it were little more than lanes, and there was no thoroughfare suitable for any sort of triumphal procession. At Cripplegate, on the other hand, there was a broad road running along practically all the northern border of the city, with the defensive wall and ditch on its left and a region of gardens, orchards and what Stow calls 'fair houses of merchants' on its right. The London Museum copper-plate map, already mentioned, shows a considerable part of this area, and it is still traceable on modern maps under its name of London Wall. In earlier days, when the Wall was still looked upon as a defensive fortification, the space within it had been deliberately kept clear of buildings, and it is not to be wondered at that the new Queen took this route, past Moorgate, All-Hallows-in-the-Wall, Bishopsgate and Mark Lane, to spend a week in her Tower of London. The palace buildings, at the south-east corner, have all been swept away, but the great water-gate is still to be seen under St Thomas's Tower. To that water-gate she had been rowed as a State prisoner in her half-sister's reign, but when she now embarked, as Queen of England, on 5 December 1558, to be borne up-river to Somerset House, she went openly to her Royal Barge, as a Queen and a free woman, from the landing-stage on the Tower Wharf.

Even the small map (*Fig. 1*) shows us how much resemblance there is between the river-front of our own day and that of the sixteenth century. The river had then no formal embankments on either side, but the view from mid-stream is curiously timeless, even today. Buildings tall against the sky shut off the main bulk of the city that lies behind them, there are still wharves and cranes and derricks and ships loading and unloading in the lower reaches, while higher up, towards Westminster, embankments and public gardens have replaced the gardens and water-gates of the great private houses of the Strand. There is no longer open country round Lambeth Marsh, and the great bulk of South London now lies behind the river-front of Bankside, but the traveller on the Thames finds plenty in his surroundings to remind him that London is a great port and a great commercial city. Vast cranes still tower on the south bank, though to a height far beyond that of the Elizabethan cranes that were once to be seen upon the north, while the name of Three Cranes Wharf still commemorates those earlier pieces of machinery, and they are shown clearly enough (*Fig. 7*) in Hogenberg's maps, both large and small, each crane mounted on an axle like a post-mill, with a surprisingly modern-looking little hut to shelter the windlass and the lifting-gear of the jib.

Fig. 7 *The Three Cranes in the Vintry: detail from the* Civitates *map*
(London Museum)

One great feature of the Thames is gone, however, after an existence of over six hundred years. It was only in the last century that the stone piers of old London Bridge were finally demolished, and the bones of its twelfth-century founder scattered among the unwanted and unrecorded dust. The timber superstructure, with houses running its whole length and sometimes making an actual tunnel of the roadway, had gone many years before, but the architects and engineers of the Middle Ages had known their work and done it well, and the piers had stood firm on their great boat-shaped starlings, till the needs of a growing city called for a wider thoroughfare to take the ever-increasing flow of traffic. This former feature of London appears in a sufficiency of early pictures and engravings to make possible the construction of more than one model of it in its heyday, one of the best known, perhaps, being that displayed, with other models of the sixteenth- and seventeenth-century city, in the London Museum.

The value of the bridge was of course inestimable, but at the same time it constituted a serious drawback to free traffic up and down the river. The piers and their starlings were too close together to allow for the passage of ships of any size, and Hogenberg accordingly shows us the great ocean-going craft at anchor in mid-stream in the Pool of London. The day of the London Docks had not yet dawned, and cargo was loaded or unloaded with the aid of barges and lighters, an expensive business and one that offered a variety of opportunities for pilfering. What we should now call ribbon-development was in rapid progress along both banks to the east of the Tower. John Stow, when his *Survey* was published in 1598, devoted a chapter to the 'suburbs without the walls', and recorded that in fifty years the open country between the Tower and Wapping had given place to 'a continuall streete, or filthy straight passage, with Alleyes of small tenements or Cottages . . . inhabited by Saylors and victualers', and Hogenberg shows us the beginning of it, with one 'Beere house' between St Katherine's Hospital and the waterside, and another one almost opposite to it on the Southwark shore.

What the map does not show, however, and what we have to bear in mind when thinking of Elizabethan river-traffic, is the tide. The Londoner who wished to go up-stream or down, in a hired wherry, was well advised to choose a time when the set of the stream would do some of the scullers' work for them; otherwise, the journey would be continually against the current, so that it would involve more work, take more time and consequently cost more money.

Indeed, if a question of 'shooting the Bridge' were involved, it might mean an enforced wait until conditions were such as to let it be done with safety. The narrow arches prevented a free and even flow of the incoming or outgoing tide, and in consequence the bridge lay across the river like a mill-dam pierced with so many sluices. When the tide was going out, the water rushed through them to the lower level of the Pool; when it had turned, and the incoming flood met the rapids under the arches, it could be very dangerous indeed. Elizabeth herself had been taken through those rapids at an unsafe moment when she was a prisoner; so anxious were those in charge of her to get her into the Tower without more ado, that they were prepared to risk her life and their own rather than wait for the waters to run more smoothly. It is not surprising, then, that just before her coronation, in January 1559, when she could choose her own time, we read that 'Hir Grace shot the Bridge aboute two of the clocke in the afternoone, at the still of the ebbe' when she came back to stay a night or two at the Tower before going solemnly through the City, where fantastic and allegorical tableaux and 'pageants' were displayed in her honour at Fenchurch Street, Gracechurch Street, Cornhill, Cheapside and Fleet Street, to the farthest western boundary at Temple Bar. Thence, leaving London behind, she passed by way of the Strand and Charing Cross to the neighbouring city of Westminster, where next day she was solemnly proclaimed and anointed Queen, the crown being set on her head by the Bishop of Carlisle.

An illuminated initial letter (*Fig. 8*), on a State document in the London Museum, contains a portrait of the twenty-five-year-old Queen as she appeared at the beginning of her reign. Her face is full and round, with a marked resemblance in shape and colouring to those of her father Henry VIII and her great-grandfather Edward IV—each of whom, in his day, was renowned for personal beauty—and her red-gold hair flows loose about her shoulders from under the rim of her crown, in the conventional unbound tresses of maidenhood. The crown itself is worth more than a moment's attention. It is a low, helmet-like diadem with a rigid lining under its intersecting arches, and a finial that, to modern eyes, may seem disproportionately small. Yet it is just such a crown that surmounts the Royal Arms in the north-west corner of the *Civitates* map; just such a crown, again, that is shown on the head of Henry VII—the first of all the pictured monarchs to be portrayed with any attempt at a correct likeness—in the first edition of Holinshed's *Chronicle;*

c

Fig. 8 *Elizabeth in 1559: from an illuminated initial* (London Museum)

and just such a crown that forms the head-dress of Edward the Confessor in the famous manuscript known as the Islip Roll, in the library of Westminster Abbey. Differing as it does from the conventional crown-forms of the time, it seems to be an attempt to reproduce the helmet-like shape of an eleventh-century Saxon crown, and to represent that Crown of St Edward which was then still preserved at Westminster and has handed down its name, and possibly some of its actual metal, to the present coronation crown in the Jewel House of the Tower.

The Abbey where Elizabeth received her crown is to be seen on the western border of the map, and once again the ground-plan of 'the Corte' is not so very different from what we can see nowadays. The open fields are covered with streets and houses, and the country cross-roads at Charing has given place to the traffic of Trafalgar Square, but the broad thoroughfare of Whitehall still runs down from there to the gates of the Abbey and of Westminster Hall, and the old Tilt-yard of the palace, clearly shown with the central barrier running down the greater part of its length, is partly preserved for us in the enclosed fore-court east of the Horse Guards' Parade. Comparison of Hogenberg's map (*Fig. 1*) with the modern street-plan of the same area (*Fig. 2*) will show how much has remained, in spite of the Great Fire three hundred years ago and those other conflagrations that many of us can still remember, to link Elizabethan London with the London of today.

CHAPTER TWO

Londoners
at Home

On the south side of Holborn, overlooking the subway to Chancery Lane underground station, rises the Elizabethan frontage of Staple Inn (*Fig. 9*). Built about 1586, it is a very fine example of the type of town architecture that Tudor London had taken over from the Middle Ages. A framework of timber, like a great cage, towers up tier upon tier, presenting its gables to the street, and with each tier jutting out slightly beyond the one upon which it rests. Between the studding-posts—the close-set vertical uprights on each storey—are tall, narrow spaces, which the builder could turn into window-openings or close with panels of wattle and daub, adding a coat of thick plaster on the outside and quite possibly a lining of wainscot within. In the next reign came the practice of using diagonal brickwork 'nogging' to fill these spaces, but the Elizabethans followed the practice of their forebears and still worked in their old medium of stout wickerwork plastered with clay, or with a mortar stiffened with sand and horsehair so that it became something akin to reinforced concrete. A house designed after this fashion was not unlike a large constructional toy, for the timbers were cut to the requisite measure in the saw-pit and delivered on the site ready for setting up in accordance with the design. House-timbers have been found with serial numbers marked on them to ensure their being used in the right order, and it was thus possible to take a half-timbered house to pieces, if necessary, and set it up again somewhere else.

There are old houses in Chester and in Shrewsbury that were so transferred, and a famous London instance, in which Shakespeare was personally concerned, was the removal of the Theatre—which James Burbage had built and named in 1576, when it was the only

17

Fig. 9 *The north front of Staple Inn, Holborn* (National Monuments Record)

one of its kind—from Shoreditch to the South Bank. The original lease had expired, the ground landlord's terms for renewing it were exorbitant, and Burbage's sons, Richard the tragedian and his brother Cuthbert, combined with Kempe the comedian, Shakespeare, and three of their colleagues, to rent a piece of ground in Southwark as an alternative site. To the surprise and annoyance of the ground landlord—who had hoped to gain possession of the building—they arrived at the Theatre in the Christmas holiday of 1598, with workmen, hammers and crowbars, and knocked it to pieces. Like Nehemiah's men at the rebuilding of Jerusalem, they worked with swords ready at hand to prevent interruption, the beams and fittings were carted away to be ferried over the river to Bankside, and by the following summer the old timbers of the famous Theatre had entered on a new lease of life indeed, and their playhouse reopened its doors as the still more famous Globe. Looking at the cage-work of Staple Inn, one can understand how the principles of its construction made such a work of transportation possible.

Elizabethan builders used plenty of oak. William Harrison, in his *Description of England*, published as an introduction to Holinshed, makes the point that in his own time oak had come into general use, whereas in former days it had been used only for shipbuilding and as the framework for churches and the palaces of princes and noblemen, the ordinary building-timbers being willow, elm and the like. He is inclined to consider the change a sign of decadence, maintaining that 'when our houses were buylded of Willowe then had we Oken men, but nowe that our houses are come to be made of Oke, our men are not only become willow, but a great many altogither of straw, which is a sore alteration'. At the same time, he notes three great improvements in the standard of living, which had occurred in the course of a generation or two, namely the increased use of chimneys, the greater comfort of bedding, and the use of pewter for household vessels instead of turned wood. Evidence of this improvement exists in the frequent finds of bowls and spoons made of pewter, or that near-brass alloy called latten, that have been turned up in London excavations and are preserved in the Guildhall Museum. Earlier examples had been known, but those of the Middle Ages had belonged to wealthier people than Harrison had in mind—people whose spoons would now be made of silver, while pewter and latten would be appearing on the tables of those whose parents had been content with wood.

Sideboards and cupboards in the wealthier houses would be draped with Turkey carpets, and on these would be set out the family's array of plate, partly for ornament and partly to augment the illumination of the principal room by serving as reflectors behind the candles on the board. Fine glass from Venice, spring-driven clocks from Germany (made to lie face-uppermost on the table and looking rather like metal caskets), flat, brass-hilted table-knives from Flanders and tall, white stoneware drinking-cans from the Rhine might all be seen in the house of a well-to-do Londoner, particularly if he himself, like so many of his fellows, were engaged in trade across the Channel with Flanders, the Low Countries or Germany. There might even be furs from the shores of the Baltic, if he had shares in a venture round the capes of Denmark, where all vessels passing through the Sound had to heave-to and pay customs duties under the gun-batteries of Elsinore. The Departments of Metalwork and of Ceramics at the Victoria and Albert Museum show splendid examples of Continental plate, glass and stoneware, such as might have adorned the living-rooms of a wealthy citizen; and in the Guildhall and London Museums are the fragments of countless others that must unquestionably have done so, since they were dug up, centuries later, from London earth within and without the official boundaries of the City.

The Moorfields map (*Fig. 5*) affords unexpected corroboration of Harrison's remark about the increase in the number of brick or stone chimneys. On Moorgate itself, and on more than one house in the neighbourhood, the outlines of hearths with chimney-flues above them can be seen *outside* the wall, showing that they had not formed part of the original structure, but were later additions, made to bring the building into line with a less rigorous standard of living. The fire would no longer be built in the middle of a main hall, under a central louvre through which the smoke might eventually find its way to the open air, but on a hearth, under the draught provided by a proper flue; and the hearth itself might be ornamented by a fire-back of iron, possibly cast in Sussex or the Weald, with a design of figures, appropriate heraldry or, perhaps, the householder's initials with the date of his marriage or the setting up of his house.

The provision of chimneys made it easier for different rooms to have their own individual sources of warmth. Some of them were still heated by tiled stoves, after the fashion of those used in northern Europe. The tiles were covered with smooth green or yellow glaze, and ornamented with figures and armorial or architectural designs in low relief. Various museums can show whole or fragmentary specimens from different parts of London: the Guildhall Museum has a complete, unbroken example, decorated with the royal arms and cypher of Elizabeth, and a broken tile in the same collection bears a recognizable likeness of the Queen herself. The large stoves, of course, were permanent fixtures, and it is not surprising that there was a demand for something smaller as well, which could be carried about. This demand was met, in the late fifteen-sixties, by one Richard Dyer, who had learned in Spain 'the making of earthen furnaces, earthen fire-pots, and earthen Ovens, transportable', and who set up a kiln outside Moorgate, where he taught their manufacture 'and for a time enjoyed the whole profit thereof to himselfe by Pattent', as Howes usefully tells us in his edition of Stow's *Annals*. Specimens of these practical little hand-stoves are still extant, the London Museum owning a simple but virtually unbroken example in earthenware (*Fig. 10*) with the characteristic green glaze of the period, while the British Museum possesses an interesting variation, namely a candle-sconce of yellow earthenware in which a panel with the Queen's arms, badge and cypher rises up like a reflector behind a semi-circular tray with sockets for two candles, and with perforations in both borders to suggest that the object was originally fitted with a wire guard.

Fig. 10 *Hand-stove of green glazed earthenware* (London Museum)

Dyer was not the only man to apply foreign technique to the production of home-made luxuries. As the reign went on, it became increasingly possible to obtain, from London craftsmen, commodities that had formerly needed to be imported from abroad. It was no longer necessary to look as far as Venice for fine glass with its characteristic moulded ornament. First, manufactories of glass after the Venetian fashion had been established in the Low Countries, and presently the enterprise of Jacopo Verzelini led to the setting up of a glass-house in London itself, in the buildings of a suppressed friary south of Fenchurch Street. Unbroken specimens of Verzelini's work are of the greatest rarity and value, but the Victoria and Albert Museum possesses a notably fine example (*Fig. 11*), engraved —presumably to commemorate a wedding—with the names of John and Joan Dier and the date 1581. The Guildhall and London

Fig. 11 *Engraved drinking glass by Verzelini, 1581* (Victoria & Albert Museum. Crown Copyright)

Museums have fragments of this so-called Anglo-Venetian ware from various London sites, the latter collection containing the stem and foot of a wine-glass, of characteristic Venetian form and moulded with a design of lion-masks, dug up in the street that still bears the name of Crutched Friars. The furnace at 'the glass-house' was popularly supposed to be kept perpetually burning, and on

Sunday 4 September 1575 the whole factory caught fire. Though the Lord Mayor, Sheriffs and Aldermen 'practised there all meanes possible by water buckets, hookes, and otherwise to have quenched it', it was only the fact that the old hall of the friars was stoutly built of stone, Stow tells us, that prevented the conflagration from spreading farther afield and doing widespread damage among the wooden-built houses of London, as a more famous conflagration was to be doing in that neighbourhood ninety-one years later to the very day.

Furniture, still, was of the simplest. Stools and chests formed the most usual seating accommodation, with a chair, perhaps, for the master of the house and, if space permitted, there might be a high-backed settle in the chimney corner. In the latter part of the reign there arose the fashion of having chests inlaid with elaborate architectural designs, usually depicting, somewhat impressionistically, the windows, gables and turrets of Nonsuch, the Queen's fantastic palace in Surrey. Like the painted *cassoni* of Renaissance Italy, these chests were suitable containers for bed-linen and other household textiles, and specimens in more than one public or private collection show that the design was obviously a popular one.

Elizabeth's accession had been hailed as inaugurating a period of peace and prosperity after the anxieties of life under Mary and her Spanish king-consort, and there are signs that this wishful thinking was by no means unjustified. Like the fine glass of Venice, the small table-knives of Flanders were soon superseded by their London-made equivalents. Richard Mathews of Fleet Bridge obtained in 1563 a ban on the import of knives from abroad and is recorded by Stow as 'the first Englishman that attained the perfection of making fine knives and knife hafts'. Moreover, we are indebted to Stow or to Edmund Howes, who brought out an augmented edition of the *Annals* after the old chronicler's death, for a marginal note that enables us to identify them. The records of the Cutlers' Company do not afford us any particulars of Mathew's mark, but in the margin of Howes's edition of the *Annals* we find the information that he 'attained his skill by travailing, and residing in divers nations', and that 'His Knives were marked with the halfe moone, according to his letters patents'.

Other useful innovators and benefactors of those early years are commemorated in the same pages. A negro in Cheapside in Queen Mary's reign used to make 'Spanish' (i.e. steel) needles, but would never show anyone how he did it. Now, however, the art of needle-

23

making was being taught—doubtless to the great joy of tailors and housewives—by a German immigrant named Elias Krauss. Elizabeth herself, in the second year of her reign, had for the first time experienced the delight of wearing knitted silk stockings, made for her by one Mistress Montague her silk-woman, and had declared that she would never again be content with the tailor-made cloth hose that had been, till then, the general wear for courtiers and commoners alike. A few years later, the Earl of Pembroke became the first nobleman to wear knitted stockings—not of silk, but of worsted—after an apprentice named William Rider had borrowed a pair from an Italian visitor, had examined them and started making others like them, to be retailed by his employer, Master Thomas Burdet, 'over against Saint Magnus Church' by London Bridge. Many years later still, in 1599, the matter was taken a stage further by a Cambridge Master of Arts called William Lee, who 'devised and perfected' a method of knitting stockings and other garments by machinery, and obtained a patent for it from Henri IV of France before sending out his representatives into other foreign countries to spread this new labour-saving device throughout the civilized world.

The ordinary amenities of life found their own ways of improvement. Fine holland had been the usual wear in the way of good body-linen, and the Moorfields map (*Fig. 5*) shows how the laundresses were accustomed to spread it out on the grass to dry after washing it in the running water that was so easily available just outside the city. Soon after the silk stockings, however, there came in another minor luxury in the shape of fine cambric and lawn. It was thinner, softer and more comfortable than the material that it superseded, but it would have been too limp for ruffs and wristbands had not the Queen 'made special meanes for some Dutch woman that could starch'. London was filling up, just at that time, with Protestant immigrants from the Netherlands, and one married couple went into the Queen's service carrying their special crafts with them. William Boonen brought in the use of coaches, then a complete novelty, and was duly appointed Her Majesty's Coachman, while his wife was employed as Starcher to the Queen. Elizabeth's example was followed, as usual, by many of her subjects. Coach-owning and coach-building increased, but at first affected country life only, not that of the town. Clear-starching, however, was another matter, and was wanted everywhere.

In 1564 a couple of Flemish refugees named Van den Plasse came to London, and Mistress Dinghen Van den Plasse set herself up in business as a clear-starcher. Her first customers, naturally, were her own compatriots, but soon the superior quality of the Netherlanders' linen attracted the attention of the more exacting London house-wives. At first they made up their own ruffs, of cambric or even of fine lawn, and sent them to Mistress Dinghen for starching, but as time went on they sent their daughters to her for instruction in the craft. For twenty shillings she would teach a pupil how to boil starch; the more elaborate instruction in its actual use cost four or five pounds, and the popularity of the new fashion is attested by the extent to which moralists were still denouncing it and preaching against it nearly twenty years later, when the Puritan Philip Stubbes brought out his *Anatomie of Abuses* in 1583. So numerous are his allusions to the wearing of fine lawn and cambric, so intemperate his invective against the 'devil's liquor', starch, that the reader comes away with the conviction that, whether or not the fashions were sinful, they were certainly popular. Indeed, by the irony of circum-stance, they were especially popular among the Puritans themselves, many of whom came from religiously-minded Dutch or Flemish families, and who looked on these starched caps and collars as clean, decorous articles of their national dress.

Another general benefactor at the beginning of the reign was John Rose of Bridewell, a maker of musical instruments and deviser of the bandora, a kind of flat-backed lute which some musical historians have claimed as the ancestor, in name as in general con-struction, of the American banjo. He was father and namesake of a still more famous son, who made stringed instruments of many kinds and whose patrons included the Queen herself. Music played a great part in the Elizabethan Englishman's life. Ability to sing a stave at sight, and to play with some degree of accuracy on lute, viol or recorder, was considered to be part of an ordinary citizen's education. If he found himself waiting his turn at the barber's, there was usually a cittern or bandora hanging there for him to strum, he could take his part in a madrigal with his family or his guests, or in a catch with his companions at the tavern. He would not come near the skill of the professional singers or instrumentalists who were among the paid staff of a nobleman's household, or the violence and versatility of the ballad-singers whose extensive and largely un-edifying repertory earned them a livelihood among the less fashion-able. He played or sang as a true amateur because it gave him pleasure to do so, and to do so well enough to give pleasure to others.

25

And, quite possibly—almost certainly, if he came of a family of Dutch, Flemish or Huguenot refugees—he and his household would sing psalms together as part of their daily family worship. Even Stubbes admits that 'if musick openly were used . . . to the praise and glory of God, as our Fathers used it . . . or privatly in a man's secret Chamber or house, for his owne solace or comfort to drive away the fantasies of idle thoughts . . . it were very commendable and tollerable', but he has no good word for its 'beeing used in publique assemblies and private conventicles, as a Directorie to filthie daucing', and when he comes to discuss professional performers and teachers of it, he launches out into a passage of intolerant invective that is too long, and perhaps too strong, to cite in its entirety, and too rich in its eloquence to suffer curtailment or expurgation.

Without being as thorough-going a Puritan as Stubbes, the average Londoner was still a decorously religious man. His sons, on getting up in the morning and being washed, brushed and generally tidied, would wait upon their father in his shop or counting-house and receive his blessing before setting off for school. At the family meal, it was their place to sit bare-headed, while their father and any guests of consequence wore their hats at the board, and to serve their elders with food before settling down to their own, possibly at a smaller table. One of them might be called upon to read to the company, from the Scriptures or from some other 'work of edification', and the same boy or another would say grace at the beginning and perhaps the end of the meal. (It is a point of interest that at school meals, on the contrary, the boys were instructed to keep their caps on, to guard against the dropping of stray hairs into the soup or pottage.) Knives and spoons would be the work of London cutlers and pewterers respectively, forks were regarded as peculiar objects used by foreigners abroad but quite unsuitable for the Englishman's dinner-table. Court ladies, perhaps, and slightly eccentric noblemen, might care, now and then, to impale fruit or sweetmeats on these curious little two-pronged bodkins, but the Elizabethan Englishman, even if he had become accustomed to the table-manners of the Continent, was advised to forget them on his return, abandoning alike, in the words of Fynes Moryson, the fork of Italy and the affected gestures of France. It is to the courtier's table, rather than to the citizen's, that we may most probably assign those charming sets of wooden roundels, like table-mats, that remain in various public and private collections, some of them with the original carved and painted boxes in which they were kept. They were used as trenchers for fruit, cheese or cakes, which were eaten off the plain side, and were then turned over for scrutiny and appreciation of the flower-girt 'poesies'—facetious rather than refined—that were to be read upon the other side, resembling in tone the flippant or sentimental mottoes found in old-fashioned Christmas crackers.

The average London merchant was accustomed to dine at noon and to sup at six in the evening. His table was generously but not extravagantly furnished. On formal occasions, such as those feasts represented nowadays by the Livery dinners of the great City Companies, all possible splendour and elaboration were employed, and the rarest delicacies were sought out and set upon the board; but at home it was customary for the householder to have only three or four dishes to choose from, and sometimes even to have one day's hot joint served up cold for a later meal. He liked to have his bread as new as it could be without being oven-hot, and his beer as old as it might be without being sour. Wine and beer were habitually stored in the cask, and drawn into flagon or tankard when required for the table, but the Dean of St Paul's, Dr Alexander Nowell (compiler of the Church Catechism and formerly Headmaster of Westminster School), had lately discovered, and introduced to humanity at large, the virtues of bottled beer. The story is well known, and recounted in Fuller's *Worthies of England*, how 'leaving a bottle of ale (when fishing) in the grass, he found it, some days after, no bottle but a gun, such the sound at the opening thereof', and stoneware beer-bottles of the sixteenth and seventeenth centuries are familiar objects in many museums. The early examples were made in the Rhineland, but the royal arms on some of them show that these had been made especially for export to this country. Characteristic of them all is the practice of decorating the front of each with a bearded mask in low relief. First of all the face was that of a grave, square-bearded German merchant, the silver lid of the vessel completing the picture by simulating the flat, round citizen-cap, but as time went on the beard became round or pointed, and the expression turned into a cheerful grin, as on a fine London Museum example (*Fig. 12*) dated 1591. In the following century the mask became cruder and more disagreeable in aspect, and by the second half of the seventeenth century it was vaguely supposed to be a portrait of the Duke of Alva, Governor of the Spanish Netherlands, but the 'D'Alva bottles' of the Restoration appear to have been known merely as 'greybeards' or 'the man with the beard' in their

Fig. 12 *Stoneware 'greybeard' bottle, dated 1591* (London Museum)

earlier days. The theory that they were meant to be portraits of Cardinal Bellarmine, and to satirize the rotundity of his figure, is a mid-nineteenth-century suggestion and has no evidence to support it. According to Fynes Moryson, who met him, Bellarmine was a thin little man with a wispy beard, and these full-bearded, jolly bottles were flourishing before he had risen to any degree of fame—possibly, even, before he was born.

But some of these new discoveries, as the reign went on, sank gradually downwards in the social scale. Despite the patronage of the Dean of St Paul's and the Earl of Pembroke respectively, bottle-ale and worsted stockings are associated, in the plays of Shakespeare, with contemptuous objurgation. To Doll Tearsheet, screaming insults in a pothouse in *The Second Part of King Henry IV* Pistol is a 'bottle-ale rascal', and several other things as well, while King Lear's faithful Earl of Kent, when quarrelling with Goneril's unpleasant steward, calls him 'a base, proud, shallow, beggarly, three-suited, hundred-pound, filthy, worsted-stocking knave'. Coaches, too, had become more numerous and popular by the end of the century, and intensified the dangers and difficulties of the London streets. The narrowness of the roadway, and the virtual impossibility of widening it by destroying or diminishing the areas of house- or shop-property on either side, have been discussed already. Now, when the citizen's wife claimed to ride in her coach as easily as the country gentlewoman, the practice of driving four-wheeled vehicles within the compass of the city walls made it all the harder to deny entry to carts and drays bringing in produce from the countryside. Stow has left us an expressive word-picture of the complicated traffic problem that was arising, with fast-driven coaches and slowly-moving drays combining danger and obstruction and increasing in number all the while, so that 'the world runs on wheels', he says, 'with many whose fathers were glad to go afoot'. Not for the first time, and certainly not for the last, Progress was proving itself to be rather a doubtful blessing.

 # *Market and Supermarket*

From its very beginnings London seems to have developed along the lines of a market, increasing rapidly in size and importance from the bridge-head market that it must originally have been when the possibility of carrying a bridge-borne road across the tidal river established the site as the first great cross-roads of England. Stalls in a market differ from shops in a town or village in one important particular, for they look for their custom to the visitor from outside, not solely to the resident round the corner. One consequence of this is that the craftsman or merchant finds it advisable to display his wares in close proximity to others of the same kind if he is to attract the notice of his particular public. A visitor in search of plate, for instance, will readily look over the stock of several goldsmiths in the same street or quarter, and make his purchase after due consideration and comparison, but he may lack the time, the energy or the desire to go farther afield on the chance of finding what he wants in a different quarter of the town. In some of our older market-towns, and indeed in certain London street-markets, the practice is observable to this day.

Many remaining street-names indicate the nature of the business formerly carried on there. Westward from the Mansion House runs a thoroughfare still called the Poultry, though even by Elizabethan days the poulterers who gave it its name had been succeeded by grocers, haberdashers and upholsterers. The church of St Mildred-in-the-Poultry, with its weather-vane like a three-masted vessel, has been swept away, though its name remains in the alley called St Mildred's Court; the lock-up, known as the Poultry Compter, that stood four doors away from it, has vanished entirely, but Grocers' Court and Grocers' Hall, the headquarters of that great City

Company, are still to be seen hard by, in the district where the Elizabethan grocers once had their shops and stalls.

Westward again from the Poultry runs Cheapside, one of the few really wide streets of early London. It was not so much a thorough-fare as a market-place, a great, central, open space where goods of all kinds could be displayed on stalls, or the stalls themselves be cleared away to leave the ground free for a sporting event such as a joust, or the dubiously edifying spectacle of a public execution. Like many a country market-place, it was dominated by a cross, and was also the site of a public fountain. Indeed, the column known as the Standard seems to have served both functions. From an unrecorded date it had been, like a market-cross, a central landmark and the natural place for proclamations, executions and the burning of condemned documents, and in the fifteenth century, when it had become very ruinous and had needed to be repaired, there was mention of a conduit in it which had to be rebuilt likewise. This was the oldest of the Cheapside monuments in Elizabethan times, a still older Standard, farther to the west, having been demolished in 1390.

The more famous Cheapside Cross was not part of the City's fabric at all, but was one of the series of memorial crosses put up by Edward I to mark the stages in the funeral procession of his dearly-loved queen, Eleanor of Castile, from Hardeby in Lincolnshire to her tomb at Westminster. Part of it, with finely-carved shields of the arms of England and of the Queen's native Castile and Leon, is still extant, and is now in the Guildhall Museum, but when the Cross was standing in Elizabethan Cheapside it had undergone changes that had altered it considerably from its original appearance. It had been renovated with new lead-work in the fifteenth century; been gilded, burnished and gilded again in the sixteenth, the last occasion having been in 1554 to grace the arrival of Queen Mary's consort, Philip II of Spain; and in the succeeding reign had lost favour and come to be regarded as a survival of idolatry and, what was more serious, an obstruction to traffic. More than one proposal was made for its removal in the cause of Progress, but all were unavailing, and the Queen's monument still towered, among its surrounding images, in the middle of the road. Then, one June night in 1581, some persons unknown, moved either by Protestant zeal or exuberant hooliganism, broke some of the lowest range of statues, including figures of the Risen Christ, the Virgin and Child, and Edward the Confessor. A reward of forty crowns was offered for information about the offenders, but no one earned it. The figure of the Virgin

31

D

had been hauled from its position with ropes and leaned dangerously out over the roadway, the Child had been removed and the arms that held him had been broken, and in this precarious and unsightly state the monument appears to have remained for over fourteen years. It is just possible that Stow himself knew rather more about the episode than he chose to set down in print. In his *Annals* he tells the story with one or two more details than appear in his *Survey*, such as the explicit statement that the damage was done by 'certain young men' who barricaded the street with ropes on both sides of the Cross and started by trying to haul the statues from their places. When this proved impossible they broke the arms of some of the figures and removed the Holy Child entirely, and in spite of the proclamation and reward 'nothing came to light, for every one of them kept others Councell, till their dying dayes'. It seems likely that the whole episode grew up from the strong feelings aroused by the rumours of a possible marriage between Elizabeth and the Duke of Anjou, brother of Henri III of France. The French King's commissioners were staying in Whitehall at the time, to make arrangements for the marriage, and popular feeling was running high against it, so that this outburst of image-breaking may well have been one of its manifestations.

It had long blown over by 1595, when there was trouble for a different reason, once more on a Sunday in June. Some disorderly youths on Tower Hill threw stones at the local officers of the peace, organized themselves under the encouragement of an ex-soldier with a trumpet, and drove the officers back as far as Tower Street. The Sheriffs arrested the trumpeter and a number of the rioters, and that evening the Lord Mayor, with the City Sword borne before him, rode to Tower Hill to see that all was quiet. Unfortunately some of the Tower warders, and the servants of the Lieutenant of the Tower, took exception to the carrying of the Sword on the debatable ground covered by the Liberties of the Tower. The resultant scuffle was quieted by the tact of the Lord Mayor, but the news of 'these and sundry other disorders committed in and about her Citie of London' drew forth a stinging rebuke from the Queen, with a warning that if the appropriate officials did not keep better order they would be not only dismissed from office but punished as accessories to the fact. It is surely no mere coincidence that the City decided to show its loyalty by keeping the following 17 November, the anniversary of Elizabeth's accession, as 'a day of great triumph, for the long and prosperous raigne of her Majestie' and by putting some of its monuments into better order. Paul's Cross, that famous outdoor pulpit, was repaired and painted, and partly surrounded with a brick wall, and at long last a start was made with the ill-used Cross of Cheapside. The leaning Virgin was put back in her proper place, and in the following year a new Child was placed in her arms.

Stow does not appear to have thought much of it, as he disrespectfully calls it 'a new mis-shapen Sonne, as borne out of time all naked', and adds that the other saints remained broken as before. The Resurrection scene on the eastward side was replaced by a small shrine of grey marble containing an alabaster figure of Diana with Thames water 'prilling from her naked brest', but it does not seem to have been very long before this in turn went out of order. We may safely assume that by 1599, when Shakespeare was writing *As You Like It*, the vicissitudes of Cheapside Cross had become a standing joke, and that any London audience, hearing Rosalind speak of weeping 'for nothing, like Diana in the fountain', would think primarily of that recent and not over-successful experiment in municipal hydraulics.

Things were still happening to it in the last years of the century. The woodwork of the cross-shaped finial became rotten, and its lead casing began to bend, making it once more an object of potential danger to the passers-by. The whole monument was surrounded with scaffolding, the decaying cross was taken down and it was proposed to replace it with an obelisk—or, as the Elizabethans called it, a Pyramis—an architectural ornament that was coming into fashion. A message from the Privy Council, however, informed the Lord Mayor that the Queen disapproved of the substitution. The monument was a *cross*, and it was to be repaired as such, 'and placed again as it formerly stood'. The attempt to modernize it had been successfully checked, but nothing was done about restoration and the monument stood headless for the space of a year. Then came a still more peremptory order from the Privy Council that the work was to be done, and done at once 'without any further delay . . . respecting especially the Antiquity and continuance of that Monument, ancient Enseigne of Christianity'. This could not be ignored. A wooden cross, sheathed in lead like its predecessor, was set up on the summit and gilded, the stonework was cleaned and the scaffolding removed, and in less than a fortnight the iconoclasts had been at work again, damaging the figures of the Virgin and Child almost as badly as before. After that, however, came the revolt, arrest and execution of the Earl of Essex and his accomplices, and for many weeks there were extra guards and watches kept in the City, while the common sense of the Londoners was enough to show them the unwisdom of stirring up trouble when any sort of disturbance might be misconstrued as rebellion. The battered old monument with its gilded apex was allowed to remain more or less undisturbed and, as *Fig. 13* shows, it still retained much of its Elizabethan appearance when it was finally demolished in 1643.

Fig. 13 *Cheapside Cross in its last days: from* The Downfall of Dagon, *1643* (London Museum)

The Cross and the Standard are indicated on Hogenberg's *Civitates* map, but on too small a scale to give any real impression of their appearance. The larger section, engraved on copper, and depicting the eastern side of the City immediately below Moorfields, does not extend far enough westward to include them, but it is able to illustrate, in the roadway between Bow Church and the Poultry, a small castellated tower of stone, which was another important feature of Cheapside. If the Standard is the equivalent of the market-cross, the Conduit in West Cheap might well claim to be the parish pump. It was the principal source of the water-supply in the market, and it drew its water not from the Thames, like the Diana fountain, but from the country heights of Paddington. As far back as the thirteenth century, Paddington 'sweet water' had been conveyed underground, in pipes of lead, to a leaden cistern, and the Conduit had been rebuilt and enlarged by Thomas Ilam, one of the Sheriffs, in 1479. Now it served not only stall-holders and visitors to the market, but customers farther afield. Hogenberg has indicated the fact by illustrating, on his City copper plate, a group of tall, tapering vessels (*Fig. 14*) rather like jugs in appearance. He has made them nearly as big as the Conduit itself, and indicated certain details of

Fig. 14 *Stalls and water-vessels in Cheapside in about 1560: detail from the City copper plate* (London Museum)

their construction, so that there is no mistaking what they are. The shape, the handles and the horizontal bands carefully indicated on each, all combine to show that they are water-cans, tall, narrow, wooden vessels hooped with osier, used by professional water-carriers to bear fresh water from house to house, where they sold it to housewives who had neither the time, nor the wish to fetch it for themselves from the fountain-head. The London water-carrier seems to have had all the reputation for lively familiarity, gossip and general garrulity associated with milkmen and tradesmen's boys in later years and natural to a regular house-to-house visitant. If

35

Jonson's *Every Man in his Humour* is anything to go by, he was readily accepted as a 'character', since the water-carrier's part in that lively comedy seems to have been cut to the measure of the important comedian William Kempe.

Turning back for a moment to the detail from the City copper plate, we may notice another interesting feature of Cheapside, immediately adjoining the Conduit. It is a rectangular block, which looks at first sight like a long, low marquee with a flat top, but a closer examination shows that it is built up in sections and is not in fact a single building at all. It is a collection of stalls, with their tables, corner-posts and canopies, packed closely together in the middle of the street and ready to be shifted out at market-time and disposed along the wide thoroughfare like similar stalls that are displayed in today's London street-markets and in many a country-town. Lydgate, the monk of Bury, in his satirical poem *London Lack-penny*, had given a lively description of a countryman's first experience of the London markets of the early fifteenth century, and his account of the combined effect of crowds, noise, high-powered salesmanship and miscellaneous thievery would serve very well for the markets of Elizabethan London and not too badly for some of the street-markets of the present day, where shoppers and sightseers jostle one another among the stalls, and the various vendors are in high rivalry in their attempts to catch and hold the attention of the passers-by.

In addition to the stalls, the map gives an indication of the appearance of the regular shops. Hogenberg's artist seems to have made his drawings on holidays or after closing-time—not un-naturally, if he were to have space and leisure to draw at all—so the shop-boards are not set out before the windows and adorned with goods for sale, but again and again, before the house-fronts, he shows the posts and crossbars on which the boards—possibly the actual window-shutters—were supported to serve as display-counters when the shop was open. Above the doors and ground-floor windows, likewise, he shows the continuous penthouse or canopy that might run along a whole street-front and would serve to shelter the goods on show from sun or rain. When trade was over for the day, and the shop shut up, the projecting penthouse might still serve to guard the passer-by from a sudden downpour, as it does in *Much Ado About Nothing* where Conrade and the drunken Borachio take refuge under just such a covering and discuss their affairs in the hearing of the Watch, or in *The Merchant of Venice*, where Gratiano and Salarino wait in its shadow for Lorenzo's arrival to elope with Jessica. Usually it was a permanent fixture, but now and then there were hinged canopies, which could be let down at night to close the shop-front. To shelter under one of these might mean trouble for the unwary, as is learned by Black Will and Shakebag—surely two of the most inefficient murderers in literature—in the anonymous *Arden of Feversham*. In the course of one of their futile attempts to murder the unfortunate Mr Arden they lie in wait for him under cover of such a penthouse, until the shop-boy closes the premises for the night, presumably by taking away the struts that propped up the canopy, so that the shutter comes down and hits one of the would-be assassins on the head—a piece of broad comedy in the Laurel and Hardy vein that must have been all the more enthusiastically welcomed because it mirrored an easily imaginable hazard of Shakespearean London.

The whole episode occupies only a few lines, but throws a new light on certain London ideas and practices. The apprentice declares that it is time to shut up his stall to avoid pilfering by the crowds coming out of St Paul's—an interesting reflection on the types of people likely to visit the Cathedral. Black Will, nursing his broken head, calls to Shakebag to draw his sword, but the apprentice is more than ready to stand his ground, boldly answering 'We'll tame you, I warrant', and Arden the intended victim, passing by with a friend, pauses a moment to look at the scuffle but is hurried away by his companion, who assures him that the brawl is probably a put-up job intended to attract a crowd and give someone else an opportunity for picking pockets. Finally the injured bully, still whining for compensation, is threatened with a beating and the jail by the truculent apprentice, and goes out discomfited, muttering threats against the shop-signs, as less likely to hit back if he assaults them. The apprentice element in the audience must have enjoyed the scene and warmly applauded the creditable behaviour of its representative.

To the north of Cheapside and the Poultry, the visitor would have his ears assailed by continuous and particularly unpleasing noise, for in Lothbury lay the establishments of the metal-founders who cast round or cylindrical objects such as candlesticks, spice-mortars and the like and then gave them their final polish by turning them on treadle-lathes under the file or rasp 'to make them smooth and bright, with turning and scratting (as some doe terme it) making a loathsome noyse to the by-passers', as Stow expressively puts it.

37

Shakespeare's Hotspur, whose jokes are usually centred on the northern part of the City, talks of hearing 'a brazen canstick turned', when comparing offensive sounds, and the local audience, going to see him at the Theatre in Finsbury Fields, would have every reason to know what he was talking about. The Founders' Company had its hall in Lothbury, just to the west of St Margaret's Church, and water 'in great abundance' was piped from Hoxton and Islington to a conduit set up in 1546.

For, in spite of the congestion and narrowness already mentioned, London was full of these cisterns, wells and open streams, not yet silted up or defiled with rubbish. Thames water was still sweet and considered eminently fit for drinking, so that certain wealthy citizens had it laid on to their houses. The stream of the Walbrook, running right through London from Moorfields to the Thames, was not yet vaulted over through all its length, and there was a tradition that it had been navigable by barges as far north as Bucklersbury. The Elizabethan city still had unexpected gardens lying behind the house-fronts here and there, and the city churchyards provided further open spaces, even within the walls. From time to time the digging of a new grave might cut into an old one, for the day of individual headstones had not yet arrived, but any bones thus disturbed would be removed and stacked in the charnel-house belonging to the church. It was only in later years, and under different burial-methods, that the churchyards of London reached the state of congestion and decay so expressively recorded by Dickens and his contemporaries.

Most of the large buildings, such as Guildhall itself and the halls of many of the City Companies, dated from the Middle Ages, but one characteristic Elizabethan building of particular beauty was, and is, the Hall of the Middle Temple (*Fig. 15*). The four Inns of Court—Middle Temple, Inner Temple, Lincoln's Inn and Gray's Inn—were in fact colleges for students of law, and were actually referred to, in Elizabethan and immediately post-Elizabethan times, as 'the third University of England'. Each of the Inns had very much the constitution and buildings of a college, save for the fact that the Middle and Inner Temple, instead of having individual college chapels, worshipped in the old church of the Templars, whose premises they now occupied.

Middle Temple Hall was built in 1572, and is a magnificent specimen of an Elizabethan 'great hall'. The general plan is that of the halls of the Middle Ages—a dais at one end for the High Table

Fig. 15 *Interior of Middle Temple Hall* (National Monuments Record)

and a partition at the other end to screen off the passage leading to the kitchen, the buttery and the servants' quarters—but though the form is medieval, the spirit of the Renaissance has everywhere controlled its decoration. The screens, the panelling, even the pendentives of the mighty hammer-beam roof are all made vehicles for ornament in the classical style, as that style was understood by the artists and craftsmen of the sixteenth century. What was originally thought of as the necessary woodwork of a stone building has now become decorative as well as functional, and has given a new richness to an old-fashioned architectural form. It has escaped the Great Fire, it has endured attack from the air and undergone damage from enemy bombing, but it still survives, and the visitor can look round at walls and timbers under which *Twelfth Night* was performed in February 1602. Indeed, if it was the Chamberlain's Men who were engaged to give the performance, rather than merely to make the text available to a company of legal amateurs, then that panelling may have echoed the voice of Shakespeare himself.

The Young Gentlemen of the Inns of Court were not Londoners in the strictest sense of the term, but nevertheless they formed a striking feature of the London scene. As has been indicated, they represented what might be called the undergraduate element, being 'gentlemen of blood', supposed to be undergoing a legal training and subject to various disciplinary ordinances by the Benchers of their Inns. Their quarters lay just outside the official boundaries of the City, their apparel was nearer that of the citizen than that of the courtier, since they were forbidden to wear swords, high boots, cartwheel ruffs and similar extravagances of fashion, and they were in an excellent position for getting involved, on occasion, in the equivalent of a University 'town and gown' imbroglio. When considering Elizabethan London, therefore, we must always bear in mind the existence of this high-spirited, keen-witted collection of young men living just outside the walls, continually associated with the City to the point of familiarity, but never actually belonging to it or sharing its responsibilities. The students of the Inns of Court were often hard-working young men, for all their flippancy, but their industry was apt to lead them to positions, and duties, with which the London citizen was not directly concerned, for it was in the neighbouring city of Westminster that they might hope to find permanent and profitable employment, at or about the council-board of their Sovereign or in some branch of the judiciary, centred on Westminster Hall.

The one great public building raised in the City itself during Elizabeth's reign was the Royal Exchange on Cornhill. Previous to its erection, there had been no central business headquarters in which London merchants could meet and discuss professional matters in general. The halls of the individual gilds or companies were the private property of the bodies that operated them, and were not open indiscriminately to the representatives of all trades or crafts. Lombard Street, for a long time the accepted gathering-place of the merchants, was getting too small for the increasing commercial population of London, and the general rendezvous was gradually transferred to a large public building that was perforce open to everyone—the nave of St Paul's Cathedral. Though highly unsuitable on ethical grounds, it was so convenient that there was quite an old-established tradition of its use for the purpose of miscellaneous commerce. In the Middle Ages people had been prosecuted on various occasions for selling fish in it, and by the middle of the sixteenth century it was the unofficial business-headquarters of London. Retail trade might be suppressed, or at least discouraged, by vigilance and severity on the part of the responsible public officers, but it would be more difficult to check meetings between grave persons of consequence who might be discussing problems of theology or questions of parish government, rather than such worldly matters as the price of corn, wool or liquor, or the state of the markets in general. One pillar was an unofficial gathering-place for masterless men in search of employment—it was there that Sir John Falstaff engaged Bardolph, although there was already a proverb against buying 'a horse in Smithfield, a servant in Paul's or a wife out of Westminster'—and a tomb, erroneously supposed to be that of Humphrey, Duke of Gloucester, was haunted by persons whose financial position would not allow them, just then, to dine at their own expense. Their presence in the neighbourhood of the monument was a tacit indication to better-furnished friends that they were available to accept an invitation to dinner, and to 'dine with Duke Humphrey' was a current phrase for picking up such an invitation or going hungry if none were to be had.

This was not a state of things that would commend itself to the self-respecting London merchant, or be shown, without awkward explanations and apologies, to important business-visitors from abroad. What was wanted was a London counterpart to the Antwerp Bourse, a general clearing-house for all commercial matters, where merchants could meet and discuss their personal and national

41

affairs with rather more comfort and dignity than the current rough-and-ready arrangements allowed. Accordingly, the City authorities bought up a considerable amount of house-property on Cornhill, cleared the site by selling the houses that stood on it to 'such persons as should take them downe, and carry them thence', and handed the cleared space over to Sir Thomas Gresham, a distinguished mercer, diplomat and financier, for the erection of a Bourse at his own expense, to supply the City's pressing need. The view of Cornhill in the Hogenberg plate, and Stow's above-cited words about the sale of the houses, combine to show that the superseded buildings were timber-framed structures after the old fashion, capable of being demolished, removed in pieces and re-erected elsewhere, but the new Bourse was good, solid mason's work, with a covered walk like a cloister surrounding a central stone-paved quadrangle, which was open to the sky. Hogenberg has engraved a famous view of it (*Fig. 16*), showing the central quadrangle with its cloistered walk around, and the many weather-vanes, in the form of Gresham's badge of a golden grasshopper, that surmounted the chimney-stacks at the

Fig. 16 *The Royal Exchange: as engraved by Hogenberg* (British Museum)

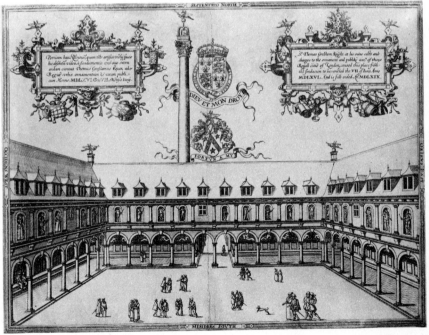

corners and the tall column on the northern side, as well as the tower of the gatehouse on the Cornhill front.

While the courtyard and the arcades were a general meeting-place for merchants, the upper floor, known as the Pawn, was designed to be a gallery of shops, so that retail trade could be carried on upstairs while the fluctuations of the wholesale market were being discussed, or directed, by the influential merchants in the courtyard. Gresham's idea was a new one, and meant a complete departure from the market-principles that had hitherto influenced London business. Instead of streets and districts devoted to special trades, he was trying to establish a general shopping-centre, or supermarket as we should now call it, where merchandise of many kinds could be seen and purchased without an elaborate journey round the different quarters of London associated with this commodity or that.

At first, this revolutionary proposal was regarded with hesitation. There was no rush to take space in the new building, and for some time the greater part of the Pawn stood empty. Then matters came to a head when arrangements had to be made to receive a visit from the Queen. It was imperative that the new building should appear at its best, as the centre of a variegated and flourishing commercial enterprise, and at the same time it was to the interest of the shop-keepers who had rented premises in the Pawn to display their wares as widely and elaborately as possible to this important visitor and her suite. Gresham himself went round the Pawn twice in one day, interviewing the individual tenants and putting forward a mutually convenient plan, by which they should have a year's rent-free tenancy of as many shops as they could furnish, fill with goods and light with wax candles. As the annual cost was normally forty shillings per shop, that was a considerable saving, and the success of the venture is shown by the fact that the tenants found it worth while to keep on their premises when they had to pay rent for them, and even when that rent was raised, eventually, from forty shillings to ninety.

The royal visit duly took place: Elizabeth dined with Gresham at his house in Bishopsgate Street, returning afterwards by way of Cornhill to inspect the new building, and finally 'caused the same *Bursse*, by an Herald and a Trumpet, to be proclaimed the *Royall Exchange*, and so to be called from thenceforth, and not otherwise'. Gresham's building was destroyed in the Great Fire, and replaced by a structure that was independently burned in 1838, but the stone pavement of the original Elizabethan quadrangle is still in position

43

in the middle of the present Royal Exchange, and for many years the galleries around it housed, appropriately enough, the exhibits of the Guildhall Museum.

Lombard Street had practically ceased to be a centre for general business, merchants were meeting instead in the more spacious quarters provided by the new building, and there was an interesting variety of retail business going on upstairs. Milliners, armourers, apothecaries, booksellers, goldsmiths and glass-sellers are all recorded as having premises there, and Howes, when editing Stow's *Annals* in the reign of Charles I, proudly claims for the building that 'now it is as plenteously stored, with all kinds of rich wares and fine commodities, as any particular place in Europe'. The milliners or haberdashers seem to have dealt in what we should now call fancy goods, as they sold mousetraps, birdcages, shoehorns, lanterns and Jew's-harps in addition to the 'Milan work' of feminine adornments that gave the trade its name. The by-products are less irrelevant than would at first glance appear, for among the dress accessories that a milliner would be expected to supply were the *rebatoes*, or flat frames of silk-covered wire, which would be attached to the collar of a doublet or bodice and serve to support the cartwheel ruff of fine starched lawn. Craftsmen or craftswomen who could make these would find it worth while to employ their ingenuity in making wire mousetraps and birdcages into the bargain, and possibly those exasperating little instruments known as Jew's-harps, which are held firmly in the teeth and which turn the whole head and the facial bones into a sounding-board to echo and amplify the note of a twanging wire. Shoehorns were always useful, and were sometimes elaborately engraved, notably by an artist named Robert Mindum, many of whose signed examples are still extant in a private collection; lanterns were set not with glass but with thin plates of transparent horn, and candlesticks were not always the treadle-turned metal utensils of Lothbury, but were sometimes light open-work contrivances of wire, knotted and twisted with a variation of the familiar birdcage-and-mousetrap technique.

An interesting point about Stow's account of the Pawn is his reference to the armourers as selling 'old armour and new'. It reminds us of the various functions of armour in Elizabethan days, and the various kinds of armour required to fulfil them. There was a statutory obligation on persons of means—from £15 a year upward—to provide themselves with a certain quantity of arms and armour, graded according to income, so that they could supply their quota of such munitions in a national emergency. There was the independent (and more conscientious and satisfactory) energy of volunteer bodies such as the City trained-bands, with their musters and drill-parades at Mile-end, and such occasional functions as the local authorities might authorize, even though the Marching Watch, an elaborate procession in armour which used to go through the City from St Paul's to Aldgate and back again on certain festival-evenings in summer, had long been put down by royal proclamation as an unnecessary expense. And, it must be remembered, there was another use for armour in the great social and sporting functions of the Tilt-yard. The London merchants might have to cater for all these, and take care to have suitable wares for each.

For orders in bulk, equipping large bodies of men, trained-band volunteers and the like, the 'Almain rivet' was the most likely to be useful. This was a half-suit, of the type worn by the German mercenary infantry of twenty or thirty years before, and usually of German manufacture, with the proof-mark, it might be, of the armourers' guild of Nuremberg. It consisted of breast- and back-plates, a gorget with arm-defences reaching nearly to the elbow, and thigh-pieces stopping just short of the knee, and was in great demand because of its adaptability. As it did not involve the knee or elbow joints, it did not have to be made to measure, the back- and breast-pieces could be adjusted by the straps over the shoulders and at both sides and, within reasonable limits, it would fit almost anybody. The fact that it was old was not necessarily a handicap: an infantry helmet of the latest type could be worn with it if required, infantry tactics were very much what they had been in the days of Henry VIII, and infantry armour still had to protect its wearer in the same places, and against the same hazards, as it had done a generation before. The quality of the steel afforded the necessary protection, the design of the armour permitted a satisfying degree of mobility, and these old-fashioned 'harnesses' consequently remained in demand among those who wanted something practical and inexpensive and were not concerned to follow the latest style.

New armour could also be bought ready-made, particularly if it were of the same type, without complete arm- and leg-defences. These, for absolute certainty of fit and ease of movement, ought to be made to measure, and in fact were so made, for those who could afford it. Otherwise, an approximate fit could be obtained by altering the rivet-holes, paring off the edges of plates that were too long, or putting in extra laminations to add length to those that were too

45

short. An armourer worked very much as a garage-proprietor does today, effecting running-repairs after a joust or an engagement, replacing damaged parts either by making new ones in his own workshop or, if he could lay his hand on an incomplete or damaged harness of the right type, by stripping it of the necessary part to provide a replacement, and adjusting, reinforcing or curtailing the armour to suit the customer's measurements as easily, and as habitually, as his modern counterpart adjusts the driving-seat of a car.

The Royal Armoury at Greenwich made its products almost exclusively to measure for the exalted clients who had licence to order their armour at that famous workshop and could afford to pay for it. A folio volume of water-colour drawings in the Victoria and Albert Museum was once the pattern-book of the Armoury, and contains formal diagrams of the armour made for its customers, among whom were many of the most famous nobles of Elizabeth's court. The full-length figures are depicted in stiff, fashion-plate attitudes, but the drawings are of especial value as indications of the engraved decoration on each, and of the amount of extra pieces that made up a full harness. The nobleman who ordered his armour from Greenwich would expect, and get, something that would serve him in every capacity he could imagine. He could wear it on the battlefield or in a formal parade; he could reinforce it with special pieces for the artificial conditions of the Tilt-yard, where protection was everything and mobility a minor consideration; he could take off the leg-armour and fight on foot in different thigh-pieces (a very important consideration in skirmishing-work in the Low Countries or among the hills and bogs of Ireland); and he could wear a close-helmet with one or another kind of vizor, or an infantry steel-cap with no vizor at all, or an open-faced helmet known as a burgonet, which could have a guard for the cheeks and chin clipped or strapped on to it at will. There were plates for the peak and cantle of his saddle, there were funnel-shaped 'vamplates' to be threaded on his lances and provide cover for his hand, there were even stirrups decorated, like all the other pieces, in the individual pattern associated with this particular armour. In the Tower, in the Wallace Collection, in the Armoury at Windsor Castle and in great public collections all over the world can be seen the work of this great industry, which flourished in the sixteenth century on the very borders of London.

For those who did not aspire to own suits from Greenwich, there was other armour of varying quality, some of it imported from abroad. Sir Thomas Gresham, in his younger days, had shown his diplomatic ingenuity by smuggling currency into England in the casks containing armour officially bought for defence purposes when he was Mary Tudor's financial agent in Antwerp, and there seems to have been a good supply of armour in later years, not necessarily obtained as a cover for a rather dubious financial transaction. Possibly a certain amount had been captured from Spanish troops in the Netherlands, where the Earl of Leicester had been appointed General of the United Provinces, and had many noble volunteers serving under him. Certainly there was a lottery of rich armour held for two days in 1586, in a timber building set up for the purpose in St Paul's Churchyard; and in 1584 the authorities in Ireland, when sending back three hundred suits to the Ordnance Office as unsatisfactory, complained that this official issue, supplied to them at a cost of forty-two shillings a suit, was inferior to the armour that they could buy in London for twenty-five. The armour in the lottery two years later is described by Stow as being 'marveilous rich and beautifull'; had it been otherwise, one might have suspected the Ordnance Office of having found an ingenious way of disposing of that 'Government surplus' which had earlier been found wanting and sent back from Ireland with disdain.

CHAPTER FOUR

Londoners and their Leisure

In its merrymaking, as in its marketing, London long preserved a good many characteristics of the country-town. Stow, when writing the chapters on 'Sports and Pastimes' for his *Survey*, was able to quote a long passage by the twelfth-century writer, Fitzstephen, on the subject of London's recreations, and to corroborate it by personal recollection of the amusements of his own youth, showing that there had been very little change in four hundred years; but the rapid development of London in his own lifetime was bringing about some necessary alterations in this as in other things. Increase of business meant increase of traffic, and that in its turn meant that the open street, even when it was as wide as Cheapside or Cornhill, was no longer available to be used as a sort of village green for recreation and exercise after business hours. 'The Youthes of this City', he says, 'also have used, on holy dayes after Evening prayer, at their Masters doores, to exercise their Wasters [i.e. single-sticks] and Bucklers: and the Maidens, one of them playing on a Timbrell, in sight of their Masters and Dames, to dance for Garlands, hanged thwart the streets, which open Pastimes in my youth, being now suppressed, worser practices within doores are to bee feared'. He speaks, too, with kindly reminiscence of the time when practically everyone, on May-morning, 'would walk into the sweete meddowes and green woods, there to rejoice their spirits, with the beauty and savour of sweet flowers, and with the harmony of birds, praysing God in their kind'; though this idyllic view was not shared by Stubbes, who denounced these May-day excursions as idolatrous and improper, and took the gloomiest view of what happened to young people who went on them.

The ceremony of bringing in the Maypole, wreathing it with

flowers and dancing round it, he considered (quite correctly) to be a direct survival of heathen practices, but here he had been anticipated by the curate of the church of St Katharine Cree, who in 1549 preached vehemently at Paul's Cross against the parish maypole on Cornhill, which gave its name to the church of St Andrew Undershaft, but had not been set up for more than thirty years. The famous Evil May-day riots of 1517 had given the celebrations rather a bad name, so the maypole had been allowed to rest idle on its iron brackets under the penthouse-eaves of the street, over a whole row of shop-fronts and doors and the entrance to a close known as Shaft Alley, but on the afternoon of the sermon, the tenants of the various houses were stirred up to lift it from its hooks and cut it in pieces, each man appropriating the section that had lain across his own house-front, and most of it was burned.

Fig. 17 *The Quintain: from Stow's* Survey, *1598* (London Museum)

There was no more dancing round the maypole on Cornhill, but Stow mentions, and illustrates, a smaller structure that was set up farther to the west along the same street, near to Leadenhall. This was the Quintain (*Fig. 17*), an upright post with a crossbar turning on a pivot on the top of it. One end of the crossbar was wide and flat like a paddle, the other was equipped with a bag of sand swinging from a staple. This simple piece of apparatus provided an opportunity for emulating the performances of persons of rank and fashion in the Tilt-yard, as it called for a certain amount of skill and judgement to ride briskly at it with levelled lance or staff, hit the broad end of the crossbar smartly enough to spin it, and go on fast enough to avoid a blow from the sandbag as the arm swung round. But as Puritanism had overthrown the Maypole, so Progress banished the Quintain from Cornhill. The middle of an increasingly busy road was becoming no place for sporting events like this, and it is not surprising that Stow refers to the structure merely as a memory. On the South Bank, of course, the situation was different, and Hogenberg's map in the *Civitates* illustrates a quintain, small but quite recognizable, at the cross-roads by Paris Garden, just across the river from Blackfriars. Whether in use or not, it remained as something of a landmark, under the name of the 'turning-tree', and the open space about it was used, on occasion, for public executions.

Amusements like the Quintain, henceforth, would be best kept outside the limits of the City, and the only open-air game still occasionally played up and down the London streets was football. Stubbes fulminates against it as 'a bloody and murthering practice' in itself, quite apart from the enormity of its being played on Sundays. Making the usual allowances for his excitement and exaggeration, one is left with the impression that Elizabethan street football was very different from the elaborate and well-organized Florentine game on which Giovanni de' Bardi published a treatise in 1580. Stow associates it with 'people of meaner sort', playing in the open fields and streets, and Shakespeare, in *King Lear*, makes Kent use the term 'base football-player' when kicking Oswald the steward's legs from under him—giving an indication, incidentally, of the kind of horseplay that Stubbes had denounced, which was apparently a regular accompaniment of the game.

Once outside London Wall, there was more space for recreation, and in particular for archery. The bow had been the traditional English weapon in the Hundred Years' War, and there were many people—Clement Edmonds, the Queen's Remembrancer, was one of them—who considered archery still superior, in warfare, to the new-fangled 'shot', but it was admitted, by Elizabethan writers, that the general standard was not what it had been. The study and practice of archery had been made compulsory by law, which was itself a sign that they were no longer taken for granted as universal, and the archery itself differed from that of the Middle Ages. Harrison, in 1577, had lamented the fact that 'our strong shooting is decaied and laid in bedde', and though there was a twelve-score range in Finsbury Fields, not far from the Theatre and the Curtain, popular taste ran more to 'roving', i.e. going over a large space of open ground shooting either at random or from one to another of a series of marks.

The London Museum copper-plate map (*Fig. 5*) illustrates this very well. Just to the east of Finsbury Court, three men appear to be shooting haphazard at nothing in particular, regardless of the closeness of cows, pedestrians and the public road. Something of the same kind is going on in Spitalfields, but the eastward edge of the plate cuts off our view of the rest of the field, so that it is impossible to judge the wisdom or indiscretion of the proceeding. Behind the group of archers is a thing that looks rather like a milestone, but is presumably a mark-stone or 'standing prick', to indicate one of the points on a rover-course, and its distance from its nearest neighbour. A late Elizabethan manuscript, in the library of the Society of Antiquaries, gives a list of the mark-stones in Finsbury Fields— nearly two hundred in number—and notes of the distances between them, and it is clear from this, and from the figures of archers and spectators on the Museum plate, that a good many Elizabethan Londoners regarded archery as some of their modern descendants regard golf. At the corner of the field, by Finsbury Court, there is a group of archers (*Fig. 18*) and a spectator in a short cloak with a hood hanging at the back, a feathered hat and a sword, presumably a fashionable visitor from the neighbourhood of the Court. Just to the north of them, a citizen in the usual long gown and flat cap and a woman in a broad-brimmed hat are waiting for the men on the

Fig. 18 *Archers in Finsbury Field : detail from the Moorfields copper plate* (London Museum)

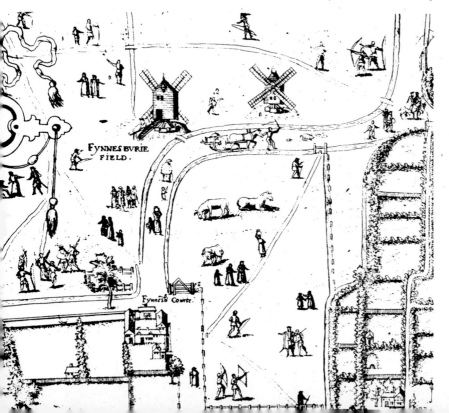

extreme left to shoot before they cross the field, and two women and a child are apparently doing the same thing on the other side. Farther north, a man with a bow in his hand is gesticulating— probably shouting—at a solitary pedestrian hurrying between the windmills and, farther north still, on the right, an archer is being restrained by his companion because an old gentleman with a beard, who has taken off his gown but is still wearing his flat citizen-cap, is plodding along, bow in hand, just where the others are about to shoot. Hard by the western windmill is another mark, and by it stands a young man holding up an arrow, as if to protest at its nearness to the places where citizens walk about for pleasure.

There are several Elizabethan references to the fatal accidents that could happen on the archery-ground or in its neighbourhood. Dame Alice Owen, as a child, got an arrow through her hat when playing in the fields, and later founded a famous school in Islington in commemoration of her escape; and when Beaumont and Fletcher had to make an end of Ralph, the comic apprentice in *The Knight of the Burning Pestle* they made him come on 'with a forked arrow through his head' and explain that he had been shot when walking in Moorfields. Such an end was a casualty that would be naturally deplored and yet felt to have something vaguely comic about it, possibly because of the ever-present suggestion of potential negligence on the part of the victim, like the various characters in an almost forgotten song called 'More Work for the Undertaker', whose indiscretions led them to a variety of sudden, violent, but not, somehow, genuinely tragic ends.

And if the bow and arrow were considered dangerous, firearms would naturally be still more so. Hard by Spitalfields, and just south of the precincts of St Mary Spital, the map shows the walled enclosure known as the Artillery Yard (*Fig. 19*). Here, with a solid barrier of bricks and mortar to keep them from injuring their neighbours, the citizens of London could practice their marksmanship by shooting at butts built up of earth or turf and each having a target fastened to its face. Two butts are seen, one at each end of the range, and it may be assumed that the practice was to shoot at one butt from the other, fix a blank target to the near butt before walking the length of the range to inspect one's score at close quarters, and then turn about and repeat the process by firing the other way. On Thursdays, according to Stow, cannon from the Tower were brought up there for artillery practice, and it can be seen from the *Civitates* map that the path from the Artillery Yard ran right past the gun-foundry of Houndsditch, a fact that would greatly facilitate the testing and proving of newly-cast pieces of ordnance.

The enthusiastic volunteers who practised arms-drill and musketry were subjected, as in all ages, to a certain amount of ridicule from those who did not. 'Do you practise at the Artillery Yard?' says Flamineo, the villain of Webster's play *The White Devil*, when his sister and her maid have shot at him point-blank with pistols from which he has removed the bullets. The porter, likewise, in *King Henry VIII*, cries out: 'Is this Moorfields to muster in?' when vituperating the crowds at the court gate; and another Shakespearean allusion is to be found in the interrogation scene of *All's Well that Ends Well*, where the malicious and cowardly Parolles, belittling the soldiership of a brother officer, says of him that 'he had the honour to be an officer at a place called Mile-end, to instruct for the doubling of files', i.e. teaching volunteers to form fours. Ralph in *The Knight of the Burning Pestle* is given the gratuitous scene of a volunteer parade at Mile-end, his inspection of his troops, and his comments on the deficiencies and condition of their equipment, being enriched with a series of unseemly but apposite double-

Fig. 19 *The Artillery Yard: detail from the Moorfields copper plate*
(London Museum)

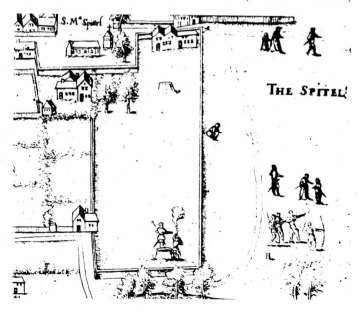

entendres. The humour is broad, cheerful and notably free from the sneers of the 'superior intellectual', so that we may reasonably conjecture that the Elizabethan attitude to these voluntary parades was not unlike that of Victorian England to the Volunteer movement, and of still more recent generations to the Territorial Army. It was legitimate, even commendable, to laugh at the absurd things that might happen in the course of this peace-time soldiering; but it is only the blackguard Flamineo and the cowardly Parolles who are allowed to sneer at the notion of indulging in it at all.

Elizabeth herself was not one to mock at the movement. In July 1559, before she had been as much as a year upon the throne, she brought the ambassadors of the Emperor and the King of France to a muster of fourteen hundred London citizens in Greenwich Park. Eight hundred of them were pikemen in corselets of steel, four hundred more were arquebusiers in shirts of mail and steel-caps, and the remaining two hundred were halberdiers in the 'Almain rivets' already described. To every hundred men there were two 'whifflers' to clear the way before them; twelve Wardens of the best City Companies rode in coats of black velvet; their six Ensigns wore jerkins of white Bruges satin, slashed and lined with black sarsanet, 'with caps, hosen and scarfes according'; and thus accoutred they paraded in battle-array before their sovereign and her official guests. In March 1572, by command of the Privy Council, the Companies saw to the equipment and training of three thousand Londoners as 'pikemen and shot'. They paraded three times a week, at the Artillery Yard for musketry-instruction and at Mile-end or St George's Fields for skirmishing practice. Stow records a fatal accident in the third week of their training, when a gunner from the Goldsmiths' Company was shot in the side with a piece of the scouring-stick or ramrod inadvertently left up the barrel of someone else's weapon. He was given a military funeral in St Paul's Church-yard, and on May-day the troops mustered at Greenwich before the Queen, and 'shewed many warlike feates, but were hindred by the weather, which was all that day showring'—a disappointing end to the season's training, as the companies returned to London that night and were disbanded on the following day.

But these parades and brief periods of training were not all. Responsible citizens recognized their importance, and as the threat of Spanish invasion increased, Londoners gave more and more of their time to the work of preparing to meet it. 'Certaine gallant, active, and forward Citizens', says Stow, 'having had experience both abroad, and at home, voluntarily exercised themselves, and trained up others, for the ready use of war', thus providing a nucleus of nearly three hundred men competent to instruct and command others in the management of halberd, pike and musket and their employment in the field. They met regularly on Tuesdays, 'every man by turn bare orderly office, from the Corporal, to the Captaine . . . and were generally called Captains of the Artillery garden', and the most famous territorial unit in the City, the Honourable Artillery Company, still turns out, on occasion, in half-armour to provide a Guard of Honour for the Lord Mayor.

Sometimes, it appears, there was a little irregular musketry, which was not confined to the brick-walled safety of the Artillery Garden. In 1579 a young man named Thomas Appletree was in a boat on the Thames between Deptford and Greenwich with a friend and two or three choirboys from the Chapel Royal. It was a fine day in July, and he had in the boat with him a loaded gun 'which hee had three or foure times discharged with bullet, shooting at random very rashly', a proceeding that might well be thought inadvisable at any time. It was particularly so at that time and place, for one of his random shots reached no less a craft than the Royal Barge, in which Elizabeth herself was taking the air upon the river in company with the French Ambassador and other distinguished personages, discussing affairs of State. France was urging the Queen to agree to a marriage with the dissolute young Duke of Anjou, while English opinion was hotly against it, fomented by the Earl of Leicester, who had long cherished hopes of marrying Elizabeth himself. His influence was great, but the French Ambassador had managed to impair it by revealing that Leicester had lately got married in secret to the widowed Countess of Essex. Elizabeth was furious, ordered Leicester to be confined in the fortress of Greenwich and talked of sending him to the Tower. There must have been consternation throughout the vessel when a sudden shot struck the waterman who was rowing next but one to the Queen and barely six feet from her, wounding him in both arms. He cried out and collapsed, bleeding, into the bottom of the barge, thinking himself to be shot through the body, but the Queen's reaction was to throw him her scarf for a bandage and reassure him with the adjuration to be of good cheer, he should not want, for the bullet was aimed at her, though it had hit him. What she said was doubtless what everyone was thinking; what she left unsaid was that if there were to be a second shot, it might well be better aimed than the first, and it would not be a

55

waterman who was struck down. But there was no second shot, a rapid investigation was made and four days later a gibbet was set up on the river-bank close to the scene of the offence, and Thomas Appletree was led out to die. In accordance with custom he made his farewell to the company, declared that he had had no thought of treason, but admitted that he had been justly sentenced, as his action had unquestionably endangered the life of his sovereign; and the hangman had settled the rope about his neck, and was ready to turn him off the ladder, when word came that the Queen had granted a pardon. More than that, she saw to it that Appletree's master retained him in his service instead of summarily dismissing him, but one may legitimately assume that that last-minute reprieve, delayed until the victim was on the very brink of death, was her repayment for those minutes of apprehension he had given her in the Barge. He would not be likely to forget, or to repeat, the indiscretions of his outing upon the river.

Other forms of amusement have left their traces on the printed page or in the very earth of London. The London Museum contains early 'woods' used for playing bowls, and some of the wooden 'cheeses'—not true spheres, but flattened on two opposite sides—that were trundled at the pins in skittle-alleys, and the indefatigable Stow has an expressive passage in which he deplores the encroachments made on the old common grounds, so that 'our Archers, for want of roome to shoote abroad, creepe into bowling Allies, and ordinary dicing houses, nearer home, where they have roome enough to hazard their money at unlawful games'. To his reasonable judgement there was nothing inherently sinful about bowls or skittles as such; they lacked, it is true, the healthy exercise and practical efficiency of archery practice or miscellaneous military training, but the real objection to them lay in the facilities for extravagant betting that they afforded to non-playing spectators. John Earle, in the following century, was to comment on bowling-alleys in which there were 'three things throwne away beside Bowls, to wit, time, money and curses, and the last ten for one', and this disadvantage drew another after it. Where the original players came merely to play, and were followed by idlers who came merely to watch, these in their turn were followed by sharper-witted individuals who came to make money by betting, and encouraging others to bet, and round the fringes of the assembly there would be a gathering of bad characters intent on picking pockets or beguiling the simpler-minded away for more drastic treatment in the neighbouring alleys. As with the racecourses, billiard-saloons and pin-tables of later years, a comparatively innocent contest, depending upon skill or chance, gained a bad name by reason of its unsavoury associations rather than by anything inherently objectionable in itself.

Londoners had a ready taste for curiosities and miscellaneous entertainments, even when there was no rivalry involved and consequently no opportunity for betting. The day had not yet come for Shakespeare's Trinculo to comment on the public that 'would not give a doit to relieve a lame beggar but would lay out ten to see a dead Indian', but there are records of certain people and things that drew audiences to see them, either as curiosities of nature or as evidence of the ingenuity of man. It seems to have been in 1581 that a Dutch giant and dwarf were to be seen in London. The one was over seven and a half feet high and twenty-eight inches broad across the shoulders, but lame of both legs, having broken them when lifting a barrel of beer; the other was only three feet high and malformed about the legs and the right arm, in spite of which he would dance a galliard, toss a cup and catch it again, perform various feats with bow and arrow, rapier, axe, hammer and trumpet, 'and drinke every day ten quarts of the best Beere if he could get it'. Both are described in detail by Stow, who, 'on the 17 of July, saw the taller man sitting on a bench bareheaded, the lesser standing on the same bench, and having on his head a Hat with a feather, was yet the lower. Also the taller man standing on his feete, the lesser (with his hat and feather on his head) went upright between his legs and touched him not'.

Stow does not tell us where these interesting characters were to be seen, or what facilities were given to the public for inspecting the curious achievement of Mark Scaliot, a blacksmith, who made a tiny padlock, key and chain small enough and light enough to be fastened about the neck of a performing flea, nor does he claim to have seen it; but he mentions the laying-up of Drake's ship, the *Golden Hind*, in a dock at Deptford, as a perpetual monument to that great sailor's achievement in circumnavigating the world, even as the gallant efforts of another explorer are recalled to modern Londoners by the sight of Captain Scott's *Discovery*, where she lies moored in the Thames off Temple Stairs. Drake's ship gradually became not only a show-piece but a place of refreshment, its cabin being sometimes utilized as a 'banqueting-house'—the Elizabethan equivalent of a modern snack-bar—but time and the visiting public

57

dealt hardly with it, patrons had a way of removing pieces of it as souvenirs (one John Davis of Deptford gave a whole chair, made out of its timbers, to the Bodleian Library), and by the time Fynes Moryson published his *Itinerary* in 1617 he could say only that 'upon the shore, lie the broken ribs of the ship in which Sir *Francis Drake* sailed round about the World, reserved for a monument of that great action'.

CHAPTER FIVE

Westminster and the Court

For some weeks of the year, Elizabeth and her court lived near to London, though not in it. The cycle of 'progresses' round the various royal estates and palaces of southern and western England would bring the Queen, for a season, to the city of Westminster, a little way up the Thames, and where the Queen went, the court and the government went with her, bringing temporary activity and well-being to a district that had fallen on penurious days. The lordly times of church patronage were gone, Westminster was no longer a community catering for, and depending on, a great medieval monastery and place of pilgrimage, religious foundations had been turned to secular uses, from the little Hospital of St James for Leprous Virgins to the splendid and elaborate palace of Thomas Wolsey, Cardinal Archbishop of York. St James's name remained, and still remains, attached to the brick walls and towers of the building that Henry VIII had raised for himself on the site of the Hospital, but the Cardinal's residence had had its very name stripped from it, and what had once been York Place was now the Palace of Whitehall.

Little of that palace was built in Elizabeth's reign, and that little did not last, but Henry's towers and walls are yet to be seen in St James's, and in the Whitehall of today stands the banqueting-house of stone that Inigo Jones designed for a Stuart king, replacing the wooden Elizabethan structure. The very ground-plan has changed, a fire in the late seventeenth century having swept away almost all the traces of Wolsey's building, but the cardinal's wine-cellar is still in existence under the ground, present-day skill having availed to move it sideways and downwards, so as to allow for the foundations of the modern buildings that now stand upon the site. The

59

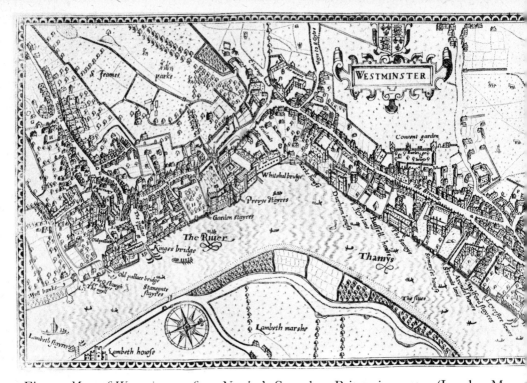

Fig. 20 *Map of Westminster: from Norden's* Speculum Britanniae, *1593* (London Museum)

Fig. 21 *Aerial photograph of Westminster today* (Aerofilms)

construction of the Victoria Embankment has set the original water-frontage a considerable way inland, so that the visible traces of Whitehall Stairs—a Tudor retaining-wall with part of a seventeenth-century terrace and staircase—lie among greensward, with roadway, pavement and parapet between them and the Thames. If we would imagine the Royal Barge landing here or at the Privy Stairs farther up-stream, we must think of a wider, shallower river, with a long, shelving foreshore at low tide, and the stairs running out into the current like a landing-stage, only to be used when the tide was right.

Paradoxically enough, the principal feature of the Tudor building that is still to be seen is an empty space where no buildings are. Comparison of the *Civitates* map with a modern map of Whitehall and the West End shows that the offices of the Horse Guards occupy almost exactly the site of the famous Tilt-yard of the palace, and the forecourt of the building, immediately behind the mounted sentries who guard the entrance-gate, is the last open space remaining from that long, narrow arena where sixteenth-century noblemen used to 'run at tilt' in splendid armour in the presence of their Queen. It was for functions like this that the Greenwich armoury designed and executed its most elaborate suits. That of Robert Dudley, Earl of Leicester, in the Tower of London (*Fig. 22*) is covered with etched designs incorporating his well-known device of the Bear and Ragged Staff (associated with the earldom of Warwick, which had been acquired by his father), the Order of the Garter and the French Order of St Michael; but the most complete and best preserved is the magnificent armour—no longer, alas, in English hands—made for George Clifford, Earl of Cumberland, as Elizabeth's personal champion. Henry VIII had enthusiastically taken part in the sports of the Tilt-yard, and his daughter, though debarred by her sex from following his example, contrived at least to do so by deputy. Sir Henry Lee was her official representative in the lists for over thirty years, only resigning that honour to Cumberland when he was sixty years old. A miniature by Nicholas Hilliard shows the new champion in his armour of purple-hued steel covered with elaborate etching and gilding, among which can be seen the Tudor rose and the initials of Elizabeth's name, duplicated back to back upon the breast, and the armour itself is now in the Metropolitan Museum of Art in New York.

Looking at the portraits of Elizabethan court gallants, in the National Portrait Gallery and elsewhere, one notices a certain

Fig. 23 *Eliza[...]
doublet, round-hose,[...]
hat and gloves* (London Mu[...]

Fig. 22 *Armour made at Greenwich for
Robert Dudley, Earl of Leicester, and now
in the Tower Armouries* (Ministry of
Public Building and Works)

resemblance between their bold elegance of outline and that of the armour just described. The impression is not an illusion: the resemblance is there, and is almost certainly deliberate. The outline of a sixteenth-century cuirass, whether made at Greenwich or in the famous armour-workshops of Italy or Germany, was designed to present a glancing surface to the point of sword or lance, and its breast-plate sloped away on each side from a central ridge, so that a thrust, however violent, would not be able to press forward and overthrow the wearer of the armour, but would be deflected to right or left. This central ridge came to a point rather below the middle of the breast-plate, and in English and Italian armour the waist-line dipped sharply down in front, the peak of the ridge overhanging it in a rounded protuberance. The German fashion continued to favour a straight or nearly-straight waist-line with the point of the breast-plate about a hand's breadth above it, and it is interesting to note that in both styles the general outline, originally carried out in steel to serve a military requirement, was soon reproduced in civilian costume. Visitors to Westminster Abbey can see it 'in the round' on the figure of young Robert Cecil (later to become the trusted minister of Elizabeth and her successor James) where he kneels on the monument of his mother, Mildred Lady Burghley. The sculptor has carefully rendered the elaborate pattern of the material, but has made it clear, at the same time, that the young man's doublet was as rigid and unwrinkled as armour, and was expected to remain so.

Examination of genuine Elizabethan doublets in the London Museum (*Fig. 23*) makes the position clear. These garments were as elegant as armour because they were designed like it, and put on like it into the bargain. The 'peascod-belly', as the Elizabethans termed it, was not only ingeniously tailored, but was customarily stuffed with horsehair, flock or bran, so that it preserved its shape unalterably and it, and the whole front of the garment to which it belonged, fitted smooth and rigid over the wearer's breast. There might be a row of buttons down the front, but only the topmost few would be made to unbutton so as to admit the head; the rest were dummies, serving merely to draw attention to the way in which all lines converged towards the peascod, giving an air of wasp-like elegance to the waist. The back of the doublet would be carefully tailored for a smooth fit, and would be lined with stiff canvas to avoid risk of wrinkles, and the real fastening of the two would be by tying-points, or even by hooks and eyes, from the armpit to the

63

F

waist-line on each side. The sleeves were quite separate. They might be tied on, with metal-tagged laces, to the shoulder-welts of the doublet, or they might be part of a garment worn underneath. Evidence of portraits, and of genre paintings like Hoefnagel's *Feast at Bermondsey* at Hatfield House, shows that sleeves, doublet and trunk-hose were often in independent and contrasting colours, so far as ordinary day dress was concerned, though for formal wear at court it was customary to wear an *ensemble* of either black or white, or a combination of the two, a fashion rapidly abandoned on Elizabeth's death.

It was not only in the breast- and waist-line that fashionable dress modelled itself on the lines of armour. From the beginning of the century, the armed man had been accustomed to protect his neck with a gorget made of hinged rings of steel, overlapping each other and fastened to supporting straps of stout buff-leather, which allowed the head a certain amount of movement. When this was first introduced in armour, the contemporary civilian doublet still had a low, square neck with a filling of lawn gathered into a band about the throat, but as the ruff became more and more elaborate, it needed stronger support than its own starched 'sets' could provide. The high steel gorget, reaching practically to the angle of the jaw, was recognized as having a becoming outline, and was duly imitated in the material of the doublet. As a result, the ruff was borne up higher at the back than in front, so that its plane followed the line of the jaw from the occiput to the point of the fashionable beard. It served to frame the face and set off the shape of the skull—it was a period when hair was worn short, especially at the back—and survived longest in Spain, where it was still in vogue in the succeeding century. Ben Jonson, writing in *The Alchemist* in 1610, describes a gentleman's Spanish costume in the words:

> He looks in that deep ruff like a head in a platter,
> Served in by a short cloak upon two trestles

—and sums up, in those two lines, the general silhouette that had been aimed at, in English fashionable society, some fifty years before. Boldness and simplicity of line, and absence of broken folds, were what characterized it, and this can be seen not only in portraits and occasionally in sculptured figures on tombs, but on actual specimens of Elizabethan costume. The London Museum contains examples of men's dress of the time, showing three different forms of leg-wear. Men who had long legs, and were proud of them, contented themselves with trunk-hose, which were little more than a padded ring round the hips, to which the long stockings were sewn; while others might wear *Venetians*—rather narrow-cut breeches fastened at the knee and sometimes distended with vertical rolls of padding down the inside of each side-seam—or padded round-hose with short, tubular extensions called *canions*, of stout fabric, which gave more and warmer cover to the thighs than the sewn-on stockings alone. The short cloak, it will be seen (*Fig. 23*), is ingeniously assisted to flare sharply from the shoulders by having a broad band of embroidery, stiff with gold and silver thread, running as a border round its lower edge, while similar decoration on the cloak itself is restricted to a series of narrower bands running from collar to border like the spokes of a wheel and serving in their turn as a stiffening framework to keep the folds regular throughout.

The outline of a doublet may be taken from armour, but the stance is very different. Busks, padding and bombast are all arranged to give the wearer a square-shouldered uprightness of carriage, but this uprightness is not to be found either in the splendid armours from Greenwich or in the ordinary 'Almain rivets' that could be purchased at the Exchange. A fighting-man, whether on horseback or on foot, requires not only protection but mobility in the management of his weapons and his horse, and his armour has to be designed accordingly. When both hands are in active use, or are held in readiness for active movements, the shoulders come slightly forward, and the head and neck are inclined a little forward likewise. In this position the muscles are at rest, and yet are at a sufficient degree of tension for instant movement when required, and for this position, consequently, armour was designed. The Earl of Leicester's armour in the Tower would not allow him to take up the attitude shown in his picture in the National Portrait Gallery (*Fig. 24*), but it has an attitude of its own, suggesting the possibility of rapid movement from its position of ease. It is noteworthy to see, in the Tower and elsewhere, how often the natural attitude of a completely armed figure resembles that of a boxer or an athlete poised in readiness for sudden action.

Leicester's portrait illustrates another feature often associated with the Elizabethan man of fashion. It was a common practice to arrange even civil dress to suggest military associations, and one way of doing so was to assume some detail associated with the wearing of armour, or at least the process of putting it on. A man might be painted in doublet and hose of rich fabric but wearing a gorget of

65

Fig. 24 *Robert Dudley, by Zucchero* (National Portrait Gallery)

steel, as if the rest of his armour were just round the corner, ready
to transform him from courtier to captain 'with the swiftness of
putting on'; or he might give a suggestion of practical efficiency by
wearing over his doublet a jerkin of leather, not in his portrait only
but in his ordinary daily life. It would not be the practical, quilted

Fig. 25 *Pinked and slashed leather jerkin for a boy* (London Museum)

garment, of soft leather, linen or velvet, that was customarily worn under the cuirass, but a far more elegant article of attire, slashed and 'pinked' with slits and small, punched holes that enabled it to stretch and mould itself precisely to the rigid outline of the doublet worn beneath it. The London Museum possesses a plain example (*Fig. 25*), decorated with slits and small heart-shaped perforations, and presumably—from its size—made for a boy, so that it does not incorporate all the exaggerations of the fully-grown Elizabethan exquisite; though it seems to show that this type of garment was no flight of an artist's imagination, but existed in actual fact.

With regard to women's dress, the portraits show a development from the simple lines of the beginning of the reign, with gowns cut like that of the citizen's wife in the *Civitates* map, but carried out in stiffer, richer materials, to the drum-like contours of the French farthingale. Here a rigid, wasp-waisted bodice, stiff as a man's doublet and even more strictly constrained by stay-busks and lacing, is abruptly contrasted with a skirt spreading out horizontally from the waist-line and then dropping abruptly to the level of the ankle or the instep. This effect was gained largely by the wearing of a bolster-like ring about the waist, and enhanced by the addition of a pleated horizontal frill, so that the wearer appeared to be rising from the centre of a gigantic rosette on the top of a cylinder. The 'Ditchley' portrait of Elizabeth, in the National Portrait Gallery, shows the fashion at its finest and most stately, and the famous

67

portrait group known as the 'Procession to Blackfriars' gives an impression of the effect created by a whole gathering of lords and ladies in fashionable dress.

But this splendour was naturally for State occasions only. About the house, the plain stuff gown would replace the elaborate toilette of velvet or brocade, or an open gown might be worn like a house-coat over a bodice and petticoat of embroidered linen. The Department of Textiles at the Victoria and Albert Museum contains a fine collection of specimens of characteristically embroidered Elizabethan garments, with their ingenious array of trailing flowers, butterflies and caterpillars worked in coloured silks, or in the plain black wool on a white ground that made Elizabethan 'black-work' famous, and the London Museum has a bodice and petticoat in remarkably good preservation, constructed to be worn over the French farthingale already described (*Fig. 26*). The petticoat is of stout linen, cut so as

Fig. 26 *Woman's dress of linen embroidered in black-work* (London Museum)

to hang vertically, almost without a wrinkle, from the farthingale at waist-level, and is covered with an embroidered flower pattern in black, with a border running round the lower hem. Above the upper edge of the embroidery, the stuff is quite plain, gathered into a draw-string about the waist. The pattern ceases abruptly at the top of the petticoat, for the horizontal area, from the waist to the outer rim of the farthingale, is exactly covered by the carefully-tailored skirt of the bodice, which is deceptive in its simplicity, and is well worth considering in some detail.

Two seams in the back are emphasized by a ladder-like pattern of black embroidery, which opens out into a fork at waist-level to mark the insertion of a gore. But for two gores thus boldly outlined, there are no less than five that are ingeniously concealed, the embroidery having been executed *after* their insertion, so that its trailing fronds and tendrils go boldly across the almost invisible seams. As a result, the skirts of the bodice lie flat on the round, horizontal surface of the farthingale, and exactly cover the unembroidered portion of the petticoat. The soft linen of the bodice has no bones or busks, and the sleeves are cut to fit closely to the arm, but had the dress been made of brocade, velvet or thick silk, the bodice would have been boned like a corset, and the sleeves cut fuller and distended by quilting, padding or even the insertion of small hoops of cane. Looking at this dress, in all its simplicity, it is easy to see how the style could be elaborated into the gorgeous garments of the portraits, and to understand why certain great ladies—the Countess of Pembroke, for instance—retained the fashion well on into the following century instead of changing over to the style made familiar by the portraits of Anne of Denmark, consort of James I.

Here was a different world from that of the London merchant and his family. Harrison's description of it, in his prefatory chapters to Holinshed's *Chronicle*, is doubtless excessive in its praise of everyone's continued good behaviour, but the general impression is one of an establishment as gorgeous as that of the Valois at the Louvre, but a good deal more decorous. According to him, the 'auncient Ladies of the Court' would be diligently employed in embroidery, netting, winding silk, or reading the Scriptures or books of English or Continental history, while their younger companions passed the time in music and singing 'when they have leysure, and are free from attendance upon the Queenes maiestye, or such as they belong unto'.

The journal of Paul Hentzner, a German jurist who travelled in

69

England in 1598, gives us a glimpse of some of them at their official duties. On a Sunday in September he saw the Queen come out, in state, from her royal apartments to go to morning prayers in the chapel of her palace at Greenwich. Noblemen and Knights of the Garter went before, then came the Lord Chancellor carrying the seals of office and walking between the bearers of the Sceptre and the Sword, and then Elizabeth herself, dressed in white silk, embroidered with pearls, and a long train of black silk, shot with silver, and wearing a small golden crown. The end of her train was carried by a marchioness, who was followed by the ladies of the court, for the most part dressed in white, while on each side walked the Queen's personal bodyguard of Gentlemen Pensioners, now known as Gentlemen-at-Arms. The procession moved on its way towards the chapel, the Queen smiling and bowing this way and that, with a gracious word in English, French or Italian for various courtiers or foreign ambassadors, and a special favour for a Bohemian baron who had letters to present to her and for whom she stripped off her glove and gave him her right hand to kiss. The procession passed out of sight, but Hentzner and his fellow-spectators stayed to await its return, and watched, meanwhile, the next stage of court ceremonial, the preparation of the dinner-table while the Queen was at her devotions.

First came in a nobleman with a staff of office, and another with a tablecloth. Both of them reverently bent the knee three times, then spread the table, bowed again and retired. Another pair came after them, one with the staff as before, the other bearing salt, bread and a plate. With the customary genuflexions they set down these articles on the table, bowed and retired in their turn. Next came a particularly beautiful Maid of Honour—a countess, Hentzner was told—dressed in white silk and attended by a matron with a tasting-knife, a broad-bladed implement like a cake-slice of the present day. After three deep curtseys they approached the table and rubbed the plates with bread and salt 'as reverently as if the Queen herself had been present'. The actual meal was brought in by Yeomen of the Guard, wearing liveries of scarlet embroidered with the Tudor rose in gold. Twenty-four dishes in turn were received by a nobleman and set in position on the table, the bearer of each being made to take a mouthful of his particular burden from the blade of the tasting-knife, as a precaution against poison. Trumpets and kettle-drums were sounding in the hall during the whole of this ritual, after which the other Maids of Honour appeared and reverently carried in the dishes for the Queen's selection and consumption in private, and the public ceremony was over. The onlookers had not exactly seen their Queen dine, but they had seen her table made ready, her food brought in and solemnly tasted in their presence, and the reverence paid to her empty chair, after which it would be natural for them to go away with a feeling that they knew now how their sovereign lady was served, and could take the mere eating of the meal for granted.

Such was the ceremonial of court life at Westminster, Greenwich or Richmond, very different indeed from the family life of the London citizen. As we have seen, the merchant and his family observed a formality of their own, but it was a formality based on responsibility. The outward appearance of the London house was notoriously untrustworthy as an indication of its interior furnishing, or the sort of life that went on inside. Servants, apprentices, sons and daughters of the house and any casual visitors were required, like the very planets, to keep their appropriate 'degree, priority and place', under the observing and critical eyes of the master and mistress of the household, and these in their turn felt a certain responsibility to supply not only food and lodging, but some degree of training in good behaviour, to those dependent on them. The object of the formality was the training of the participants themselves, whereas the object of court ceremonial was very largely its effect on other people. Elizabeth had to live the greater part of her reigning life in public, and the etiquette of her court was regulated accordingly. She prayed in public, she 'rode abroad' in public, there was a convention that she dined in public, even though the public saw no more than the formal laying of a state dinner-table, and accordingly the ritual of prayers, 'progresses' and the preparation of the table was carried out with an eye to the spectators rather than to the central figure who was their sovereign. In Elizabeth's view it was the duty of a queen to know her people and be known of them. This practice of frequent, formal, stately appearances in public made her a familiar figure, and consequently one more easily comprehended, more fully trusted and more loyally loved than she could have been had she remained secluded behind a screen of selected or self-appointed intermediaries; while at the same time the combination of the stateliness of the etiquette with the graciousness of the individual made it practically impossible for that familiarity to develop into the kind that breeds contempt.

CHAPTER SIX

Professional Entertainment

To a great extent, as has been shown, Londoners occupied their leisure by taking exercise of one sort or another, be it on the archery-ground, the military musters at Mile-end, the less violent activities of the bowling-alley or the rough-and-tumble of street football. Alongside this, however, there has always been a large section of the public that delights not so much in doing things as in watching others do them, and that is willing to pay for the privilege. It was worth while for small troupes of actors to provide entertainment for these willing spectators, if they could obtain the necessary facilities and official or demi-official permission. The earliest London theatre site is probably the site of Clerkenwell Pump, for we hear of plays and 'Interludes' being performed there, as far back as the Middle Ages, by the clergy and choirboys or schoolboys attached to various religious foundations. Later on, after the suppression of the religious houses, the entertainment world was divided into two main sections, the private and the popular. Private entertainments would be largely amateur affairs, performed by the numerous pages, singing-boys and the like, borne on the establishment of some nobleman's 'great house', or by some group of enthusiastic law-students in the hall of one of the Inns of Court. The popular performances, on the other hand, would be given on makeshift stages set up in the courtyards of inns, by courtesy of the landlords and by the leave—or possibly without the knowledge—of the local authorities.

The London inn-yard of the beginning of the Queen's reign was not, of course, the crowded jumble of carts and coaches that it afterwards became. When four-wheeled traffic was not customarily seen in London, the patrons of the inns, and users of the yards, were horsemen, pedestrians, or muleteers with strings of pack-animals, and a crowd could stand there, and watch a group of actors on a rough-and-ready platform, without unduly disturbing, or being disturbed by, the normal traffic going in and out of the yard gates. Better seating or standing accommodation, at a proportionately higher charge, was provided by the galleries that ran round the yard and connected the rooms on the upper floors. No such Elizabethan inn-galleries are to be seen in London now, but the type is well indicated by some seventeenth-century woodwork in George Yard, Southwark, the sole remainder of the tiers of galleries that once surrounded the yard of the George Inn.

Little remains, likewise, of the plays that delighted the theatre-goers of the early part of the reign. The men who acted them were careful to have themselves enrolled on the establishment of some nobleman, courtier or person of position, thus avoiding the charge of being 'vagabonds and masterless men', which would bring them at once into the hands of the law. As the official 'servants' of this master or that, they would wear their lord's livery, or at least his badge, and claim his protection if they got into trouble with the authorities. He paid them no regular wages, and their income came from the takings of their independent performances, but he might engage them professionally, on occasion, to perform for his pleasure and that of his guests, and they would be paid for this like any other entertainers hired for the festivities. This arrangement encouraged the players to keep themselves up to a reasonable standard of performance, as anything slipshod, offensive or otherwise unsuitable might earn them the loss of their lord's favour and the withdrawal of his licence and protection. The plays they acted would usually remain in manuscript, in the interests of the players who owned them. Once a play was in print, and on sale, there was nothing to prevent other companies from buying it and performing it, either in the text as published or with variations and amendments of their own, to the detriment of the players who had originally paid an author to write it for them.

The city authorities did not look with favour on these miscellaneous inn-yard performances. As with the bowling-alleys, it was not primarily a kill-joy spirit of distaste for other people's amusement, but rather an instinctive avoidance of entertainments that were likely to collect crowds of irresponsible people who should have had something better to do with their time. The stage-plays did not, it is true, offer opportunities for betting, but they were likely to prove

73

a real pickpockets' paradise, not to mention the facilities they afforded for improper assignations. They caused crowds to collect, and where there was a crowd there might be a quarrel, and one that could easily develop into a riot, and cause trouble outside the scope of the ordinary authorities of the ward. Cases of riot came within the province of that judicial committee of the Privy Council which sat in the Star Chamber, and once the affair became 'a Star-Chamber matter', it naturally reflected adversely on the disciplinary arrangements of the ward where it had originated. It is hardly surprising that the ward officers preferred to avoid, if possible, gatherings that might lead to trouble, and to Government intervention.

Apart from that, there were two other dangers less intimately connected with the quality or morals of the audience. One was the risk of picking up one of the infectious diseases that broke out so often in London. Again and again in contemporary literature we find it held as an incontrovertible fact that the average crowd smelt powerfully and unpleasantly, and such widely-differing Shakespearean characters as Casca, Coriolanus and Cleopatra speak all alike in this, if in nothing else. An epidemic of any sort, in London, meant the imposition of a strict quarantine, the closure of places of entertainment or assembly, the disorganization of the business life on which the city depended, and the distress and demoralization consequent on a disaster for which the populace in general could see no certain cause nor cure. Ordinary regulations, and their enforcement with more or less efficiency by the officers of the different wards, might be sufficient, at ordinary times, to keep this danger at a distance; but any entertainment that could gather together an assembly of miscellaneous artisans, apprentices, ostlers, tavern-loafers and the like, jammed shoulder to shoulder with more reputable citizens, was to be suspected, and if possible avoided or suppressed, as a potential disseminator of disease.

The other risk, of course, was fire. An accident on the stage with any sensational effects of bombardment, explosion, ordinary torch, lamp or taper, or that familiar thunderous noise known in stage-directions as 'chambers shot off within', might be dangerous in any building, but doubly or trebly so in a wooden-framed inn-yard, among buildings roofed with thatch, and probably with bales and lofts of hay and stacks of dry straw somewhere about the premises. Add to that the possibility of a yard overcrowded with impressionable and irresponsible people, and the fact that the premises were

surrounded by other houses, just as inflammable and full of independent Londoners, their families and their goods, and the risk
of damage to life and property becomes immense. As the possibilities
of raising a conflagration multiplied, so the facilities for fighting it
decreased. The normal practice of getting leather fire-buckets from
the parish church, and long-shafted iron hooks to pull down
burning wood or thatch so that it could be extinguished at ground-
level, would be impossible in a yard filled with suddenly alarmed
men and women and quite possibly dominated by the shrieking of
terrified horses in the stables at the side. A whole street, a whole
ward of the city might be consumed, and the most obvious targets
for blame would be the authorities who had granted permission for
the dangerous entertainment to be given in their area. It is not
surprising, then, that the first permanent playhouses were built
outside the city walls, in places where, for one thing, the city's writ
did not run and, for another, the buildings were set in more open
surroundings and not among crowded streets, so that the congestion
was less acute and the risk of plague and fire correspondingly
diminished.

Earlier than the permanent theatres were the two circular structures known as the Bull-ring and the Bear-garden, both situated on
the South Bank of the river. Hogenberg's *Civitates* map, and the
cruder woodcut example formerly ascribed to Agas, illustrate them
both as rings of covered seats, each surrounding a circular arena
lying open to the sky. The roofs—presumably of thatch—are
supported on pillars, and though the walls are solid up to a certain
height—doubtless the level of the uppermost tier of benches—there
is nothing above that, and the timber pillars rise to the roof with
empty spaces between them, like a circular verandah. This form of
construction would be less expensive than the erection of solidly-
walled buildings, as well as affording more light to the arena and the
auditorium, and it is clear from both picture-maps that it also
offered to the outside public the possibility of peeping between the
backs of the spectators and perhaps catching an occasional glimpse
of the activities within. Each building stands in an oblong enclosure
with a large central pond between two long sheds or rows of kennels
where the dogs are tethered. Beside the Bull-ring is a building that
would seem to have been the byre where the bulls were kept, and
in the other enclosure is a smaller shed that presumably housed the
bear. A very similar shed is to be seen in the corner of an open space
called 'Giardin di Piero' in the copper map in the London Museum,

75

and it has been conjectured that this may represent the site of an independent bear-garden, since it is devoid of the trees and flower-beds so readily illustrated elsewhere on the map, and has nothing of the garden about it but the name. Just to the north of it is an entrance into Moorfields, and a path from it runs north-westwards in the direction of a long building labelled 'Dogge hous', while we know from other sources that the name Bearwards Lane was for many years attached to a turning out of Bishopsgate Street on the opposite side of the road.

The baiting of bulls was very much more widely practised, all over England. For one thing, they were more numerous than bears and consequently easier to obtain, and for another, there was a suggestion that bull-beef made better eating if the animal had been baited before slaughter, and butchers in some places were liable to prosecution if they sold unbaited beef. Bulls were baited in England up to the middle of the nineteenth century, though the practice was put down officially by statute in 1835. In different towns, up and down the country, it is commemorated by place-names, and here and there even by the presence of the iron ring, let into the centre of a market-place, to which the animal was attached by a five-yard rope. It is likely that Cheapside was the earlier site for such performances, in the days when London retained more of the characteristics of a country market-town, and that as its importance grew and its population and traffic increased likewise, bull-baiting had to go across the river, like the Quintain, and find new accommodation where it was less likely to interfere with business. Mastiffs were the dogs generally used for baiting, and experience in this kind of combat was looked upon as part of the training necessary for a good guard-dog.

Bears, having no future as edible meat, naturally remained 'on the strength' for life, and became familiar, by name and temperament, to the regular patrons of the establishment. Among the names that have come down to us are Harry Hunks and Sackerson, about whom Master Abraham Slender boasts so proudly in the first scene of *The Merry Wives of Windsor*. The 'blinded bear' that was occasionally brought into the ring and attacked by men with whips, was presumably one that had lost its sight in combat but was still retained to play a crude blind-man's-buff with the bearward's men as an interlude between the regular exhibitions of baiting, and it could still give a good account of itself, even having been known to break loose from the central tethering-stake and do damage among the audience.

Puritans inveighed against this pastime not only because of its cruelty but because the displays regularly took place on Sundays, when the greatest number of potential spectators would be free to come. Stubbes, of course, denounces it vehemently, and with more justification than he has for some of his other fulminations, and Stow himself is inclined to think it was 'a freendlie warning to such as more delight themselves in the crueltie of beasts . . . than in the works of mercie, which . . . ought to be the sabbath daies exercise', when the seats at Paris Garden collapsed, and eight people were killed, at a Sunday bear-baiting in 1583.

As with the theatrical companies, the bulls, bears and mastiffs were now and then brought to Whitehall to perform for the diversion of Elizabeth and her court, and on one occasion at least, in 1599, the Queen herself paid a visit to Paris Garden. Cock-fighting was likewise actively pursued where opportunity offered, and a special building for it at Whitehall gave its name to Cockpit Steps, hard by the present Treasury buildings, but the practice was not specifically Elizabethan. Dating as it did from the Middle Ages, it achieved its highest popularity in the London of the eighteenth century, and, though long since prohibited by law, it is said not to be obsolete in the provinces even yet.

Documents preserved among the archives of Westminster Abbey give an expressive account of the details of play-production in private. Years before the first regular theatres were built on Bankside and in Finsbury Fields, the scholars of Westminster were performing before the Privy Council, usually in the former Abbot's Hall, which is still the official dining-hall of the School. The list of expenses for a play about the Judgement of Solomon, given in January 1565, includes the binding of five copies of the play in vellum, with tying-strings of silk, one special copy being adorned 'with the Queenes Maiestie hir armes', indicating that Elizabeth herself was to be present. There was obviously a certain amount of scenery, since a painter was paid five shillings for drawing the city and temple of Jerusalem and for painting towers, and the title of the play was set up in ornamental lettering, with the names of the various houses, in red, black and gold at the cost of another shilling. Costumes were borrowed or hired from the Revels Office, and brought to Westminster by boat, a tailor was engaged for the whole day to ensure that the dresses were a good fit, and as a live baby was required for the well-known Scriptural episode, it is not surprising

77

Fig. 27 *Map of London towards the end of the reign: from Norden's*
Speculum Britanniae, *1593* (London Museum)

to find a payment of a shilling to its mother for bringing it to the
stage and looking after it. Another play, in the succeeding month,
occasioned a minor tragedy, as someone borrowed the Earl of
Rutland's velvet-scabbarded rapier and, by a most regrettable
accident, broke it; while in 1569 the *Mostellaria* of Plautus, a lively
play about a ghost-story, called for some more scene-painting and
the loan of a thunder-barrel with a payment to 'twoo men which
brawght the same and thondered', presumably by rolling iron
cannon-balls round in a cask. The room in which these entertainments took place is still a part of the school buildings, and the
performance of Latin comedies by the Queen's Scholars is not yet
entirely fallen into disuse.

In those early days, it seems, the plays performed at Court, at
school or in the Inns of Court were mostly a development of the
Moralities of the Middle Ages, with characters representing virtues,
vices or other abstract qualities. Then, gradually, came in the
practice of telling stories, rather than presenting arguments, and
the actors began to represent individual men and women, often in
plots taken from classical or romantic originals. The dramatization
of history-books was something that appealed to the citizen-
playgoer as well as to the courtier, and in 1576 London got its first
permanent playhouses, both of them being erected in Shoreditch.
James Burbage built the Theatre—it needed no more particular
name, since it was the only one of its kind—in ground which had
belonged to the dissolved Priory of Holywell, and a little later in the
same year the Curtain playhouse arose on a piece of land that had
long been called the Curtain from a supposed association with a
curtain-wall in advance of the main fortifications of the City. Both
buildings have been demolished these three hundred years and
more, but the names of Holywell Row and Curtain Road, lying to
the west of Shoreditch High Street, remain to indicate the territory
in which they stood. Ten years later, Philip Henslowe built a playhouse in Southwark, on a piece of ground called the Little Rose,
from the sign of a house that had once stood there. The theatre was
called the Rose, and is the 'Play house' indicated on Norden's map
of 1593 (*Fig. 27*), which has for us the additional interest of being
the first theatre known to have staged a play by William Shakespeare.

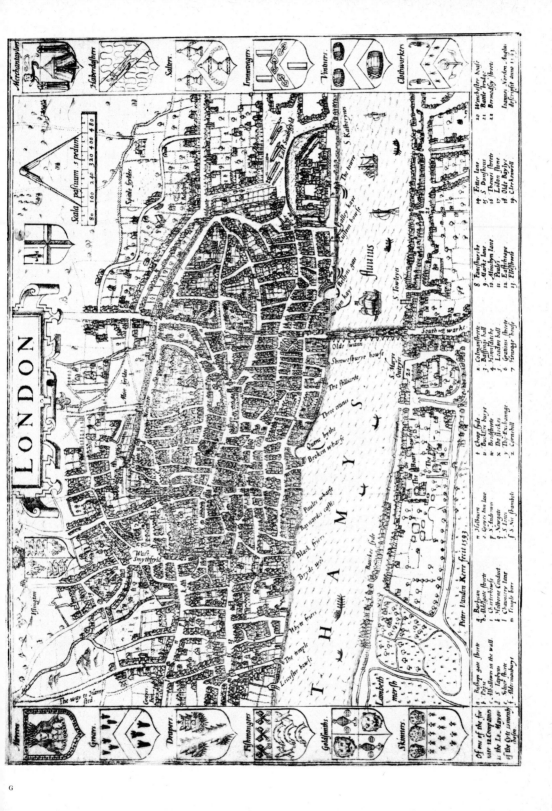

LONDON

Henslowe was not an actor himself: he was a dyer by profession, with moneylending as a side-line. He built his playhouse as a speculation, and he put money into plays as a speculation likewise. He had married the widow of his old master, and conveniently married off her daughter to Edward Alleyn, his leading tragedian and later manager of the Bear-garden. Moreover, good businessman that he was, he kept voluminous accounts, and these papers, inherited in due course by Alleyn, went into the library of Dulwich College, which Alleyn founded on his retirement. His account-books, wardrobe inventories, property lists and diary form a vast, varied and fascinating source of information about the assets and finances of the theatre, the number of plays in its repertory and the amount of each night's box-office receipts—sometimes as low as 12/6 for *Sir John Mandeville* in February 1592, and rising next week to the record figure of £3. 16s. 8d. for what appears to have been the first performance of Shakespeare's *The First Part of King Henry VI*. This play and *Titus Andronicus* are the only two of Shakespeare's to be found in the repertory of the Rose, but there is plenty of Marlowe, various works by George Peele and Robert Greene, and a famous and bloodthirsty drama called *The Spanish Tragedy*, by Thomas Kyd, in which Alleyn won wide fame as the aged and ill-used Hieronimo. Looking at the texts of all these plays we find certain factors common to most of them, notably violence of action and beauty or splendour of verbal music. Like certain popular types of television and motion-picture drama, they appeal to the senses and the emotions, rather than to the reasoning faculty. This point is important, because it helps us to understand something of the minds of the Londoners who went to them.

Very largely, the audience at the Rose must have been the same as the audience at the Bear-garden, and it is justifiable to assume, from the appeal of the plays, something of the spirit in which that audience went to the baiting of bear or bull. These early tragedies and melodramas are full of declamation, rage, battle and bloodshed, but surprisingly little deliberate cruelty. The audience is invited to be amazed, alarmed, excited, shocked, or moved with compassion, but—except perhaps in one or two passages in Marlowe—not to gloat over the sufferings of anyone, even of Lavinia, Titus or Hieronimo. In the same way, we may conjecture, men went to watch a baiting, not for any pleasure in seeing an animal tormented, but for the excitement generated by the growling, roaring, barking, shrieking and hortatory yelling that has made the name of the Bear-garden survive as a synonym for unbridled uproar, and likewise for the sheer interest of watching a fight. Very possibly they might be betting on the bear, rather than on the dogs, and it was the captive animal, not its assailants, that earned their sympathy and applause. The sport was cruel, but its patrons were not consciously so. Theirs was the simple, almost innocent, cruelty that comes of ignoring the feelings of animals or the poor, and which had given rise to the contemporary proverb that England was a paradise for women, purgatory for servants and hell for horses. It was in a later year, and for another audience in another theatre, that Shakespeare was to write the famous passage that describes Jaques, in the forest of Arden, apostrophizing the stricken deer.

With the Theatre and the Curtain, in Finsbury Fields, the position was rather different. Here, the neighbouring attractions were the archery-grounds and the place near the 'twelve-score range' that a late edition of Stow's *Survey* specifies as being generally used for wrestling. The dwellings near by, on the other side of London Wall, were the 'fair houses of merchants', such as have been already described, inhabited by people of different status, and different interests, from those who thronged the inn-yards of the city or the 'divers streets, ways and winding lanes' of Bankside. The well-educated citizen liked to do a certain amount of serious reading, and one of the most satisfying things to read was history. It was interesting, it could be edifying, and it was factual and non-controversial and devoted, at this time, to the theme that intestine strife was about the greatest evil that could come to any nation, and particularly to England. This had been the theme of Hall's famous *Chronicle* covering the period from the reign of Richard II to that of Henry VIII, and the bitter strife between the rival houses of Lancaster and York; and since Hall's death the danger had nearly repeated itself in living memory, with the troubles at Mary's accession, Sir Thomas Wyatt's rebellion and the nine-days wonder of the rise, reign and downfall of the sixteen-year-old Lady Jane Grey. Small wonder, then, that the 'pageants' at Elizabeth's accession laid special emphasis on her power to reconcile opposing factions and lead her troubled country into the paths of peace. Even so, thirty years after that accession, the Chamberlain's Men were presenting dramatized versions of the history-books that were the casual reading of courtier and citizen alike. The first Henry VI play, which had been such a success at the Rose, had admittedly drawn some of its events from the chroniclers; but these later plays,

81

covering an earlier stage in the story, had reproduced not only the subject-matter of Hall's narrative, but the ideas behind it, and had done so for an audience of Londoners who came to the theatre prepared not only to enjoy emotional passages and exciting actions, but also to think, and to consider the causes and consequences of the action as well as the deeds themselves. For such a public, then, the author had taken on the functions of the historian, and was beginning, in Sir Walter Ralegh's memorable phrase, to set before the eyes of the living the fall and fortunes of the dead.

Entertainments at these theatres were not, of course, exclusively historical and edifying. Now and then the Theatre was used for executions, and it is likewise clear from contemporary references that some people were ready to denounce any playhouse indiscriminately as a centre of vice. The 1587 edition of Holinshed inserts a quite unnecessary, and unnecessarily offensive, reference to the Theatre in an account of the earthquake of 1580 contributed by Abraham Fleming, one of the authors brought in to augment this new edition of a popular work and bring it up to date. Gosson's *School of Abuse*, in 1579, had been eloquent in its condemnation, and expressive in its description of the technique of young men when scraping acquaintance with unknown girls in the audience; this publication had been followed, a year later, by *A Second and Third Blast of Retrait from Plaies and Theaters* which called the theatre 'the chappel of Satan'; while in 1583 came Stubbes's *Anatomie of Abuses*, wherein, as might be expected, the preacher overwhelms the playhouse with his puritanical thunder, and does it, incidentally, in magnificent declamatory prose. His whole book is cast in the form of a dialogue, and shows an instinctive sense of drama, whether the author were aware of it or not. The innocent contention, by his interlocutor, that surely some plays are held to be 'as good as sermons, and that many a good example may be learned out of them', draws a retort that comes back ringing with almost Shakespearean trumpets: 'Oh blasphemie intollerable! Are filthie plaies and bawdie enterluds comparable to the word of God, the foode of life, and life itself? It is all one, as if they had said, bawdrie, hethenrie, paganrie, scurrilitie, and divelrie itself is equall with the word of God, or that the Devill is equipolent with the Lord'. Downright condemnation like this is hard indeed to answer, especially when it contains a substratum of unquestionable truth, and it cannot be denied that some plays, players and playgoers were not all that they might have been. Under the assaults of all these denunciations it might well have gone hard with the theatrical profession had not a very distinguished playgoer come into the open as its avowed patroness and champion. In 1583, the year in which the *Anatomie of Abuses* was published, Mr Secretary Walsingham arranged for the selection of twelve of the best actors from the various companies available: they were granted wages and livery as Grooms of the Chamber, and for the first time a company of players was borne on the official establishment as Her Majesty's Servants. One of them was a clown, the famous Richard Tarleton, whose cheerfully truculent features, guaranteed in their own day to raise a laugh before he had spoken a word, still scowl at us from a British Museum manuscript (Harl. 3885). Mr Stubbes, we must assume, was not amused.

CHAPTER SEVEN

The Linking of the Cities

We have seen already that the city of Westminster depended very largely on the presence of Elizabeth and her court, and that this covered only a portion of the year. As late as 1593 John Norden, in his *Speculum Britanniae*, had laid emphasis on this point, saying that the city had 'no generall trade whereby releefe might be administered unto the common sort, as by Marchandize, clothing, or such like, whereby the common wealth of a Citie is maintened', and that the three things on which they depended were the Queen's residence at Whitehall or St James's, the holding of law terms in Westminster Hall, and the periodical assembly of Parliament. All these events drew large numbers of people to Westminster and meant business for shopkeepers and miscellaneous employment for the poorer inhabitants, so it was natural for Norden to declare that 'if hir grace be long absent, the poore people forthwith complaine of penury and want, of a hard and miserable world', and to advise the citizens of Westminster to do all they could to deserve the continuance and extension of the current practice. His book gives a list of noblemen and gentlemen having houses in Middlesex, but they are almost all country places, well away from the Metropolis, and neither London nor Westminster is regarded as a residential area for persons of quality. Two contrasting figures confront one another on his title-page, as *Fig. 28* shows. The courtier, with his cloak, sword, high-crowned hat and starched ruff stands elegantly for Westminster; while the London citizen on the other side, though he has taken to the fashionable wasp-waisted doublet and round-hose, still surmounts them with the flat cap and 'guarded' gown, recalling the typical Londoner of Hogenberg's *Civitates* plate. It is clear that the difference, to Norden, was very real and very wide.

Fig. 28 *Courtier and Citizen: from the title-page of
Norden's* Speculum Britanniae, *1593* (London Museum)

Yet even as he wrote, a change was coming over London. The
Queen was growing older, her excursions about the country were
not so many, or so wide-ranging, as they had been, and her court
was gradually establishing its headquarters at Whitehall. For the
first time it was worth a courtier's while to have a real house of his
own in as close proximity as possible to Westminster; the household
and the householder were changing in their very nature, and the
courtier who had started life as a country gentleman *par excellence*
was now doing all he could to become a new kind of Englishman
entirely, namely a Man about Town. Remains of religious houses
had been given in the past to noblemen who had sold everything
vendible and had not been at all sure what to do with the remainder.
Now the properties had become what a modern land-agent would
call 'sites available for development', and developed they accordingly
were. The real burst of new planning and new architecture was to

85

come under James I, but the last ten years of Elizabeth's life saw the great change in its inception. The old bridge-head market-town had developed in its own way into a great commercial city; now it was acquiring two new features—a leisured population and a purely residential quarter. This period saw the birth of the West End.

The two cities did not become one, however, and indeed they have not done so yet. Landmarks like the obelisks in Holborn by Staple Inn, and the bronze griffin pawing his pedestal above the traffic of the Strand, remind us that there is still a difference between the City of London and the Greater London that surrounds it, for they represent respectively Holborn Bars and Temple Bar, once very real barriers by which London guarded its privileges and territory. Within the City, the police have different helmets and a different administration, the Lord Mayor takes precedence over every high official and nobleman in England except the Sovereign, and on the occasion of an official Royal visit he can, and formally does, close the route of the procession to all comers, until confronted by the one person in the land who, even in the City, is greater than he. The City Sword, symbol of his authority, is handed up to the King or Queen, is touched and handed back, and the procession moves on, but the point has been made, the existence of a boundary has been admitted, and recognition has once more been given to the privileges of the ancient city.

Certain aspects of the city must necessarily have changed with the gradual influx of this new, fashionable section of the London public. The social amenities of St Paul's, for one thing, come to the fore again. Its unofficial function as a clearing-house for business in general had been taken over by the Royal Exchange; the un-employed serving-men and the hungry 'diners with Duke Humphrey' were still at their old rendezvous, but the graver and more respectable elements of its visiting public were now to be found treading the still-remaining pavement of Gresham's new quadrangle upon Cornhill. But though the merchants of London had departed, the courtiers and gallants from Westminster came to the Cathedral in their place, to see and salute one another, to hear and discuss the latest news of domestic politics, home affairs, notorious current litigation or just plain gossip about the actions and passions of such people as were attracting general attention by their behaviour. Save for the difficulty (since the regulations of 1556) of buying drink or playing card-games in it, the Cathedral had taken on something of the quality of a West End club. The Elizabethan-about-Town would habitually look in of a morning to see who was there, and if there were any major news, any minor scandal, any interesting comment on the latest book or play, or anything in the way of a new epigram or anecdote suitable for retailing at home. By a supreme stroke of dramatic irony, it is just such a routine of fashionable triviality that Shakespeare makes King Lear, on his way to prison, imagine for himself and his one faithful daughter, when he promises her that they will:

> ... hear poor rogues
> Talk of Court news; and we'll talk with them too,
> Who loses and who wins; who's in, who's out,
> And take upon's the mystery of things
> As if we were God's spies.

Most probably Shakespeare wrote that tragedy for performance at Court; certainly its first recorded performance took place at Whitehall in the presence of King James, and the courtiers who heard those lines must have known exactly what type of fashionable and political gossip they referred to. The speech is a quiet summary of the conversations many of them heard, and took part in, when they took their customary morning stroll in 'Paul's'.

Ben Jonson, indeed, lays part of the third act of *Every Man Out of his Humour* in the aisle, popularly known as Paul's Walk, with a lively cross-section of the generality of its frequenters, including the shady Mr Shift, who explains that he has been smoking outside, and has merely come into the Cathedral to clear his throat and spit. (A passage in Weever's *Funerall Monuments* implies that people were apt to indulge in this, and even more unpleasing practices, in the dark corners behind the open doors.) In the lines of this play, written while Elizabeth was still Queen, we can trace the rise of a new and not very desirable type of Londoner, who was to become even more notorious under the Stuart sovereigns. This was the Gull, the foolish young man of fortune, who comes to town for no better reason than that everybody else does the same. Where the statesman walks in Paul's to see his friends and colleagues, the Gull walks there to be seen, and to show off his person and attire to complete strangers, mainly by extravagance of dress and behaviour. In the following reign, Dekker, the satirist, was to scarify this cult of eccentricity and ill-bred exhibitionism by writing the *Gull's Horn-book*, a burlesque manual of bad manners for the use and instruction of ignorant young men who wanted to seem fashionable, showing them how to make themselves conspicuous in public places by a calculated disregard of general decorum and the convenience of other people. The type was new to London in those days, but has since cropped up every now and again in much the same mould, and we cannot honestly say that it is not with us still.

This late influx of fashionable residents had its effect on another London enterprise. James Burbage, the builder of the Theatre and the Curtain, had very justly decided that there might be money in the idea of building an indoor theatre where plays could be produced in conditions not unlike those of a nobleman's hall. The audience would sit under cover. There would be no circus-like crowding into a central pit; the seats would be more expensive than those in his other theatres, but the company would be more exclusive in consequence. He was intelligent enough to predict that London was acquiring a new theatregoing public, consisting of elderly men who in their younger days had been students at the Inns of Court and had done their playgoing in the halls of those Inns at festival-time, or in the Great Chamber of this or that one among themselves when he called on his own company of players to entertain his guests. Burbage had already built theatres on the lines of the Bull-ring and Bear-garden for the bull- and bear-baiting public; now he was proposing to build a theatre of a different kind, on the lines of a hall in a 'great house' or in one of the Inns of Court, with a view to attracting the private playgoers likewise.

There was a very suitable site at Blackfriars. The friary itself had been dissolved, the friars had been sent about their business and the buildings had been partly demolished and turned to other uses, but the ancient dining-hall was still standing. Burbage took a lease of it and spent a considerable amount of money on converting it into a theatre, but he then found himself confronted with a development he had not foreseen. The nobility and gentry of the court were not only coming to London, but a good many of them had settled on other parts of the Blackfriars estate, and objected to having a common playhouse as a neighbour. Indeed, their influence was such that on their petition the Privy Council prohibited Burbage from opening his theatre after all. Shortly afterwards he died, a disappointed man, and his son Richard inherited a new and expensive indoor theatre, which he was not allowed to use.

The Blackfriars stood empty for some years, and at the turn of the century an ingenious Welsh lawyer named Evans took a lease of it and revived an old scheme for getting around the official prohibition. He combined with the choirmaster of the Chapel Royal, one Nathaniel Giles, to do what was being done by the choirboys of St Paul's in a private house near the Cathedral, and had been done in the past by the combined choirs of St Paul's and the Chapel Royal. This was to act on the principle that the boys of the choir might be called upon at short notice to perform a play before an illustrious audience, and that it was necessary to keep them ready for such an event by putting them through regular stage rehearsals. It was an easy step from that, to arrange that certain persons of quality might be admitted to watch a rehearsal when the production was far enough advanced to be worth seeing, and it was natural enough, in consequence, that those so admitted should pay for the privilege by making a suitable contribution towards the expenses. It was strongly maintained that these were private rehearsals and not public performances open to all and sundry. The illusion was kept up, and the money came in very satisfactorily.

When the two choirs had combined and done something of this sort in the past, the scheme had prospered for a few years until the company became involved in some rather scurrilous controversies arising out of the religious and political journalism of the time. The matter had started with the publication in 1588 of some anonymous attacks on the bishops, over the signature of one Martin Mar-prelate. The champions of the prelates tried in vain to find the source of these unedifying but entertaining pamphlets, and as they could not suppress the publications, they countered them by issuing pamphlets of their own, and commissioning suitable authors to write them. Plays were written also for the boys' company with this end in view. Martin Mar-prelate continued to issue his own booklets, but the boys' theatre had upheld the cause of episcopacy with such un-compromising and embarrassing enthusiasm that the little rehearsal-theatre had become something of a public nuisance, and had had to be closed down. Now the project was being revived, but without religious or political implications, and the Paul's Boys in the City and the Children of the Chapel in Blackfriars worked independently and in hot and lively rivalry. Each company had its poet-in-ordinary, Ben Jonson at Blackfriars and John Marston at St Paul's, and each poet wrote, and each company performed, satirical comedies that were easily recognizable as attacks upon the other. The new London public, in fact, was providing itself with a new form of entertainment.

Dekker and Jonson both had a good deal to say about the changes that were taking place in the ordinary London types. Where Dekker had scarified the behaviour or misbehaviour of self-advertising young men, Jonson cast his net rather wider, and drew up for savagely diverting criticism another type, the London citizen's wife, who was now aping the Fine Lady or developing into that terrifying monument of superficial erudition expressively described in America (when it is not being admired and imitated there) as a culture-vulture. *Volpone* and *The Silent Woman* are not, by a few years, strictly Elizabethan plays, having been produced in 1605 and 1609 respectively, but Sir Politick and Fine Madam Would-be in the one play, and the Ladies Haughty, Centaure and Mavis in the other (not to mention the redoubtable Mrs Otter, who is so severe with her husband when he mentions anything to do with the Bear-garden), indicate how certain kinds of Londoner were labouring to bring themselves into line with the new population that was to be seen at Whitehall. The old market-town was becoming urbanized under the influence of its courtly neighbour, and the old citizen-figures of the *Civitates* map were being supplanted by a generation that was certainly more pretentious but not necessarily more estimable into the bargain.

Some of the great personalities of the Court at Westminster are recalled for us by their portraits in the National Portrait Gallery and elsewhere. The Earl of Leicester we have already considered, but old Cecil is to be seen there likewise, grave and venerable in his Garter robes, Ralegh in courtly black and white, and the younger Cecil, with his little body and great brain, sitting at a council-table with old survivals like Buckhurst and Nottingham, the last two in the close caps commonly worn indoors by elderly men. In the National Maritime Museum at Greenwich—housed in a building enlarged from yet another of Inigo Jones's palaces—hangs a portrait of Drake, stout in decorous black, with a rich jewel gleaming at his waist, and in another painting hard by, dark-bearded and white-clad, is the handsome, unfortunate Essex. Drake's own jewel, a gift from the Queen to commemorate the saving of England from the peril of the Armada, is now preserved in the Victoria and Albert Museum.

The linking of the cities had led many of these great men to establish themselves on the western outskirts of London. Their houses are gone, but the sites are often commemorated by street-names or the like. The map of Westminster (*Fig. 20*) engraved for Norden's book in 1593, names and illustrates Leicester House on the river-front a little up-stream from Temple Stairs. West of that lies Arundel House, where Nottingham, the Lord High Admiral, lived and whence he was called to Richmond to attend the dying Queen in her last hours; and a building shown, but not named, between Leicester House and the Temple, is Essex House, where the Earl of Essex lived during his banishment from Court and where, after his abortive attempt at rebellion, he surrendered to the Admiral and went by river to Lambeth Palace, and thence, in due course, to the Tower and the block.

The usual form of these great houses was that of a quadrangle, with one side lying along the Strand, from which it was entered through a central archway. The main residential block occupied the side opposite to this, and backed on to a garden running down to the river, where there would be a wall, a water-gate and a flight of steps into the stream, forming a private landing-stage. Now the palaces are gone; Essex Street and Arundel Street, running southward from the Strand, give an indication where two of them stood, and the present Somerset House, though centuries later in construction, retains the name and general outline of the building that was one of the oldest and most famous of them all. The open spaces on the outskirts of the city were becoming fewer and fewer, even before the Queen's death; a royal proclamation in June 1602 had ordered the demolition of buildings that had been set up without leave, both in London and in Westminster, and in the three-mile belt encircling both, but nothing much was done, the proclamation was no more effective than others that had been made in earlier years, and Stow expressively laments that 'these Cities are still increased in buildings of Cottages, and pestered with Inmates to the great infection and other annoyances of them both'. Comparison of the map in Norden with that in the *Civitates* shows that even by 1593 there was a great deal of what we should now call ribbon-development in progress along what had been country roads both on the east and the west sides of London, particularly in Whitechapel and London. Cannon from the Houndsditch foundry are lying on the turf at East Smithfield, there are fewer trees and more houses, and two highways, which used to run eastwards among the fields, are taking on a sternly urban appearance, and are well on the way to becoming what they are now—Cable Street, Stepney, and the Commercial Road. The medieval and Tudor city is fast losing its distinctive outline and foreshadowing its later encirclement by that vast and ever-spreading perimeter of boroughs that is London-Without-the-Walls.

CHAPTER EIGHT

 *The Londoners of the Liberties*

There is another section of the London public that merits consideration, along with the courtiers of Westminster and the tradesmen of London itself. Certain localities that had once been ecclesiastical property had held, in their prosperous days, the right of sanctuary, and though this had been rendered obsolete by the Reformation, and by the dissolution of the religious houses, the tradition remained in some districts, notably those of Clerkenwell and Whitefriars. The very existence, also, of traditionally independent places like the 'Liberties' of the Tower or the Temple afforded shelter of a kind to a number of rather dubious characters—the more the better, from their own point of view, since in such a place they could gather with impunity into something like an individual colony. Within such privileged areas they were unexpectedly safe, since the City's officers were constitutionally unauthorized to follow them in, while the responsible occupants of the territory were probably unable, and might not even be particularly anxious, to drive them out. Episodes had occurred, in the Middle Ages and later, when State prisoners in the Tower had been allowed out on parole, had caused disturbances in the neighbouring taverns and had defied the ordinary keepers of the peace, knowing that their own position gave them immunity from intervention by the officers of the Ward. In the same way, as we have seen, exception had been taken to the Lord Mayor's having the City Sword borne before him when he was visiting the scene of a reported riot within the Liberties of the Tower. In places like these, and in Southwark over the water, conditions were most suitable for the housing of undesirable characters, just outside the active jurisdiction of the city in which they practised their manifold and unsavoury activities, and there, accordingly, they flourished.

In the first half of the century, the dissolution of the monasteries had led to a sudden increase in the poorer part of London's population. The monks, nuns and friars had been turned out of their homes, it is true, but they had not been rendered destitute, as arrangements had been made for them to be pensioned off. Nothing had been done, however, about the uncounted labourers, grooms, small tradesmen and other dependants who had lived in, and for, the service of the religious houses, and now found themselves without master, livelihood or known future. The new occupiers of the confiscated lands might well lack the wish, the means and the administrative power to keep up the granges or other establishments as their predecessors had done, and for many hundreds of men and women, up and down the country, there was nothing for it but to take to the road and seek their fortunes elsewhere, usually in the nearest available city or large town. Later, as the reign of Elizabeth wore on, this floating population was augmented by the addition of discharged soldiers from campaigns in Ireland, the Low Countries or the coasts and overseas possessions of Spain. Two things in this connexion have particularly to be borne in mind. In the first place, though any overseas expedition necessarily involved the transport of troops, such military service was no more than casual employment. Raids on towns like Cadiz, or organized sea-battles of any kind, were carried out by soldiers brought there for the purpose, the ships and their crews being employed solely for transport—an arrangement that led to much argument and ill-feeling, after a successful enterprise, over the apportionment of the plunder and, after an unsuccessful one, over the apportionment of the blame. Secondly, there was no such thing, in Elizabeth's time, as a national standing army. Soldiers volunteered, or were pressed, for a specific enterprise and disbanded at the end of it, and not all of them had either the opportunity or the desire to go back to honest civilian occupations. Falstaff's comments on his own troops in *The First Part of King Henry IV*, and his famous recruiting-scene in *The Second Part*, indicate how some of the rank and file would be enrolled for a campaign, and one or two grim references in *Henry V* show what was likely to become of them afterwards. If they were not hanged for military offences, they would find themselves disbanded, possibly with a final instalment of pay or a certain amount of military equipment which they could sell, and with some experience of fighting and general violence. It is not to be wondered at, therefore,

93

that so many of the more truculent among them would turn to robbery on the highway, and the less valiant, like Pistol in his last appearance in *Henry V*, to cutting purses or running houses of ill-fame.

Thomas Harman, a magistrate living near Dartford, had considerable experience of the variety of bad characters to be found in London and on its outskirts, and in 1566 he published his *Caveat for Common Cursitors*, a most useful glossary of thieves' slang and handbook of dishonest practices, primarily for the information and assistance of other justices of the peace. It found a wider public, however, and was exhaustively drawn upon by various other writers over the next half-century, with or without acknowledgement. Harrison, in the second book of his *Description*, pays proper tribute to Harman before listing his twenty-three types of male and female rogue, while the anonymous author of the *Groundworke of Conny-catching* opens his work with a few pages of possibly original composition, then blandly says: 'I leave you now unto those which by Master Harman are discovered', and reproduces practically verbatim the greater part of Harman's book. The *Groundworke* has been very dubiously attributed to Robert Greene, but must not be confused with Greene's three volumes on 'conny-catching' published under his own name in 1591-2, or his pamphlets, the *Disputation*, the *Black Bookes Messenger* and the pseudonymous *Defence of Conny-catching*, which all three came out in the latter year. These, like Harman's book, provide a wealth of entertaining information about several kinds of confidence-trick and the like, but it has been claimed, not without some justification, that they were also rather too useful as handbooks to young persons anxious to start upon a career of crime.

Dekker, in the following century, borrowed freely from Harman, reprinting Harman's dictionary of thieves' slang in his *Belman of London* and *Lanthorne and Candle-light*, similar vocabularies of later date show that the language remained the same in the eighteenth and nineteenth centuries—Borrow cites some of it in *The Romany Rye* without realizing its antiquity—and certain words are in colloquial use even now. Several phrases that are obsolete today were familiar in the days of the Regency, and one would be tempted to attribute them to that period alone, were not the works of Harman and his imitators available to show us that much of the slang was in current use in the Elizabethan underworld long before the days of Pierce Egan and his Corinthian Tom. Indeed, some may well be of pre-Reformation origin, such as *pannam* for 'bread', which is surely an echo of the appropriate passage in the Latin Paternoster, with its *panem nostrum quotidianum da nobis hodie*, now rendered 'Give us this day our daily bread'.

Shakespeare's allusions to these unedifying practices are no more than casual, but are expressive enough in the way they take such matters for granted. Falstaff and his immediate subordinates have their own channels of communication with the 'chamberlain' of an inn at Rochester, and are therefore able to hear when anyone goes by who is likely to be worth robbing. The conversation between the carriers in the inn-yard, and their opinion of the go-between, Gadshill, is merely taken in passing, as is the summary of one operation given by Pistol's boy in *Henry V*. 'Bardolph stole a lute-case, bore it twelve leagues, and sold it for three-halfpence' puts the economics of petty larceny into a nutshell.

Crime, in his view, did not really pay, All the same, Stow casually speaks of a pirate who was hanged in 1583 as wearing crimson taffeta breeches, tearing them off on his way to the gallows and distributing pieces to his friends, while one of his companions on that same last journey had already given away his doublet and breeches of maroon-coloured velvet with gold buttons and bands of gold lace. This was presumably done with a view to disappointing the hangman, who was normally entitled to claim the clothes of persons executed by him, and who made a subsidiary income by selling them afterwards. Indeed, in 1587 the common executioner, Bull, took in very poor part the instruction that he was not to have the clothes worn by Mary Queen of Scots when he beheaded her in the hall at Fotheringhay, but that they were to be burned in the hall fire to avoid any possibility of their being preserved and venerated or circulated as relics of a martyrdom. He demanded, and got, an extra payment to compensate himself and his assistant for the loss of their customary perquisite. Still more unedifying, perhaps, was the behaviour of the officials at the execution of George Brooke for treason in December 1605. The headsman demanded the prisoner's black damask gown, which he had taken off and handed to the Sheriff's man. The latter refused to give it up, whereupon the headsman refused to operate, and said that unless he got the gown, the Sheriff could do the beheading himself. The best-behaved person seems to have been Brooke, who knelt down when the time came and asked the officials to tell him the proper procedure, apologetically explaining that he had never been beheaded before.

95

H

There seems to have been a tradition of good behaviour upon the scaffold. Death by the rope was the penalty for a good many different offences, such as highway robbery, burglary, piracy, purse-cutting, clipping the coin of the realm, rape, cattle-stealing, poaching at night with masked or painted faces, misappropriation of goods entrusted to the offender by his employer, stealing a dead employer's property, and many others. Most of them were quite common, not to say popular offences, and a good many of them were elevated by their practitioners to the degree of a skilled craft, if not indeed to that of a fine art. An experienced and well-trained forger, thief or cutpurse took a pride in his work, pitting his ingenuity and agility against the officers appointed to keep the peace and, when he lost, he took equal pride in being a good loser. He might set forth a statement of repentance in prose or verse, to be hawked about in crude print as a broadsheet, or some enterprising printer might employ a hack-poet to provide an imagined confession and repentance that could come out in print as a black-letter ballad, but the ordinary English criminal was notorious for his cheerful acceptance of his deserts when the law caught up with him at last. The pirates tearing up their expensive breeches to disappoint the hangman were acting in the same spirit as the thief on the way to Tyburn who took his last drink from a benefactor's bowl at St Giles's-in-the-Fields and commented that it was an excellent drink, 'if a man might tarry by it'; and Gamaliel Ratsey, likewise—an intelligent and witty highwayman who was hanged at Bedford in 1605—pretended to have something of great importance to communicate to the Sheriff at the last moment, was taken down from the ladder to do so, talked a great deal to no particular purpose, and finally admitted that he had prolonged matters merely because he saw there was a shower of rain coming on, and thought he would like to see the Sheriff and the spectators get really wet before he was turned off the ladder and left them free to hurry under cover.

Each individual form of malpractice had its own status in the hierarchy of crime. The pickpocket, who worked without accessories of any kind, relying solely on the adroitness of his hand and fingers, was considered superior, socially, to the cutpurse, who carried a small, sharp knife and wore on his thumb a horn sheath, something between an outsize thimble and a miniature bracer, or archer's wrist-guard. The 'knight of the horn thumb' as these worthies were sometimes called, would unobtrusively advance his hand towards a well-filled purse, and with a scissors-like movement take between thumb and knife-edge the strings or thongs by which it was suspended. A slight, swift, rubbing movement would be sufficient to cut through the cord or leather, when the horn thumb pressed it against the carefully-sharpened blade, and the booty would be whipped away before its owner had time to miss it, still less to see where it had gone. Cutpurses and pickpockets frequently worked in parties, as their modern successors often do, one member of the gang being detailed to attract the attention of the intended victim by creating a diversion of some kind, and turning his eyes and his mind momentarily from the safeguarding of his own possessions. The 'nip' or 'foist' would do his share, with knife and horn or simple legerdemain, and would pass the plunder at once to another confederate, too far away from the victim to seem a possible recipient of the loot. The important thing was, and still is, to get the money quickly out of reach, so that the actual taker of it, if momentarily suspected and seized, could protest his complete innocence and submit, if necessary, to the indignity of a search, to be triumphantly vindicated at the end of it.

The varieties of crime are too numerous to describe in detail, but one or two are worth remembering for their ingenuity, such as the practice of strolling through a street by day, casting interested glances at houses or shops to see what objects of value (particularly curtains, bed-linen or other textiles) were habitually kept within reasonable distance of the windows, and coming back at dusk to fish for them with a long rod fitted with a hook on the end. The art of picking pockets was best studied in early youth, and Harman's *Caveat* gives an account of a school for young thieves conducted very much on the lines of the establishment described by Dickens in *Oliver Twist*, while Pistol's boy, in the passage already cited, explains how Bardolph and Nym, those 'sworn brothers in filching', as he calls them, 'would have me as familiar with men's pockets as their gloves or handkerchers'. A gentlemanly appearance, of course, was an asset, though not an absolute guarantee of lifelong success, for Stow records the appearance of 'one *Kerby* a Gentleman in countenance but a cousner in quality' in the pillory at Aldersgate (where he lost an ear) on 21 June 1592, and in Cheapside two days later. We are not told the exact nature of his cozenage, but it looks as if the ear-cropping had been a preventive measure rather than a specific punishment, as this would make it less easy for him, on any future occasion, to appear plausibly as 'a Gentleman in countenance', while his public exposure in the pillory at Aldersgate and in

Cheapside would have made a large section of London's public familiar with his appearance. Penalties like these were intended as marks of identification, and warnings to possible future victims, rather than as physical punishments like whipping. There was little, if anything, of deliberate cruelty in the brandings or croppings inflicted by statute for certain offences: they were the normal methods used for marking farm animals—as indeed they still are—and would naturally seem the simplest and most effective to be used when convicted rogues had to be marked in some way for the information of the public at large.

Another punishment, the loss of the right hand for brawling in the precincts of the Court, was still statutory, but was attended with so much formality, and called for the presence of so many Court officials, that it was unlikely to be imposed except in very flagrant cases indeed. For the punishment of Sir Edmund Knevet, in 1541, it had been necessary to summon: (1) the Sergeant-surgeon, with his instruments; (2) the Sergeant of the Woodyard, with a mallet and a block; (3) the Master Cook, with a knife; (4) the Sergeant of the Larder, as an authority on carving, to arrange the knife in the correct position on the joint of the wrist; (5) the Sergeant Farrier, with hot irons to cauterize the wound; (6) the Sergeant of the Poultry, with a live cock to be decapitated on the same block and with the same knife; (7) the Yeoman of the Chandlery with bandages; (8) the Yeoman of the Scullery, with a pan of fire to heat the cautery-irons and a dish of water to cool the handle-ends where they were to be held, and two benches to hold the apparatus of the various officers; (9) the Sergeant of the Cellar, with wine, ale and beer, presumably for the prisoner, the operators and possibly the supervising officials; and (10) the Yeoman of the Ewery (the Sergeant of the Ewery being absent), with ewer, basin and towels for those who required to wash. The Knight Marshal and the Lord Chief Justice were also present, the one to bring Knevet to the bar and the other to declare the sentence that he should lose his hand and remain in prison, and that his lands and property should be at the disposal of King Henry VIII. Knevet asked only that the King should pardon his right hand and take the left instead, 'for (quoth he) if my right hand be spared, I may hereafter doe such good service to his grace as shall please him to appoint', whereupon the King 'granted him pardon, that he should loose neither hand, land, nor goods, but should go free at liberty'. Harrison gives an account of the penalty, and the list of necessary officials, in his chapter on punishments for malefactors in the *Description*, implying that it was still officially current, but there is no record of its being inflicted in Elizabeth's reign. Quarrels there were, in the Court as well as out of it, but they stopped short of physical violence on the forbidden ground, though they might lead to assignations elsewhere for more private and convenient settlement.

Shakespeare's allusions to the miscellaneous rogues of London have been no more than casual, but other writers dealt with them more exclusively and enthusiastically for the sake of their own dramatic value. Beaumont and Fletcher, in *The Beggar's Bush*, treat playgoers to a display of thieves' argot with an immediate translation, and show the initiation of a newcomer into the fraternity with a ritual bearing certain disrespectful resemblances to that accompanying the creation of an Officer of Arms. But both these authors, even in their days of extreme poverty when they were supposed to have but one shirt between them, were young men of good family, observing from outside the conditions of a society to which they did not belong. Very different was their older, wilder contemporary, Ben Jonson, sometime classical scholar, bricklayer, soldier, brawler and enthusiastic ruffler in tavern society. In *Every Man in his Humour*, the play that introduced him (traditionally at Shakespeare's suggestion) to the Chamberlain's Men, and established his reputation at a stroke, the clever serving-man becomes far more than the stock trickster taken over from the comedies of Terence and Menander. Brainworm, the servant of Young Knowell (to use the English names of the revised version of the play) is a true Cockney in the multiplicity of his disguises, excuses and miscellaneous ingenuities, and his creator warms to his work as the years go by, pouring out, in various post-Elizabethan plays, an exuberant supply of characters as diverting as they are dishonest. There is no need to call in as evidence the intricacies of covetousness and double-dealing in *Volpone*; its Venetian setting may be held to rule it out for the present purpose, but there is London life enough—and very low life some of it is—in the uproarious ruffianisms of *Bartholomew Fair*, or in the situations of *The Alchemist*, where the unscrupulous caretaker makes his master's house the headquarters of a hard-working industry for extracting money from the credulous, the avaricious, the superstitious and the merely foolish. *Bartholomew Fair*, in particular, abounds in unusual and undesirable characters, like the institution from which it takes its name and in which its action is almost exclusively laid. Mr Littlewit, the proctor, visiting

99

the fair with his wife, his mother-in-law and that lady's pet Puritan preacher (a kind of Jacobean Stiggins), finds himself drawn into the booth of Mistress Ursula, the fat pig-woman, who provides roast pork—a notorious Smithfield delicacy—as well as other facilities when required in an emergency. Mr Bartholomew Cokes, a young man of more money than sense, comes up from the country attended by a disapproving and tyrannical old manservant, and falls an easy prey to the sellers of toys, gingerbread, mousetraps, ballads and the like. Matters are further complicated by the intrusions of a stray madman, and of an officious magistrate in disguise, investigating the fair in search of irregularities—or, as he terms them, *Enormities*—and the comedy goes on its uproarious way through a tangle of complications impossible to describe. But riotous and fantastic as the action is, the figures carry a degree of conviction that prevents them from being purely farcical. Jonson writes from his observation as well as his imagination, and we are left with the uneasy feeling that Messrs Whit, Knockum, Edgeworth, Nightingale and their colleagues are not unduly exaggerated representatives of London's underworld as he saw it. He is no more respectful to company-promotion and high finance, as can be seen from *The Devil is an Ass*, in which a young and inexperienced fiend begs to be allowed to practise in London for a month, but finds himself no match for the ingenuity and dishonesty of the average London sharper, and gets into such trouble that before he has been there twenty-four hours he has been cheated, robbed, cudgelled, thrown into prison and condemned to be hanged, and has to be rescued by an exceedingly angry Devil and summarily removed in a flash of brimstone, on the back of a comic demon, with the prospect of severe punishment for discrediting his profession and getting Hell a bad name.

Altogether, the London of Elizabeth, like the London of any other period, had its quota of dangerous and dishonest people, and it cannot be claimed that there was any very systematic or efficient method of controlling them. The carefully-preserved independence of the City and its democratic organization had left such control to the various Wards, each of which had to make its own arrangements about the keeping of a watch. This was the system that had been in force in the Middle Ages, and was still in force when Elizabeth was Queen. Jonson practically ignores it; Shakespeare points out some of its main drawbacks, but refrains from discrediting it entirely. The Watch in *Much Ado About Nothing* is an amateur body, given ambiguous instructions by an inefficient Constable, but it succeeds in arresting a malefactor and averting a tragedy. Elbow, the Constable in *Measure for Measure*, is a doddering old man who has no qualifications for his office, and claims none, but is paid to act as deputy for successive citizens who wish to avoid the trouble of undertaking it themselves. Against him, however, is set the figure of the Provost, an upright, humane and honest officer, as a reminder that not all public officials were necessarily venal or incompetent. It is surely permissible to trust that this character, as much as any of the others, was drawn from life, and that some such figure once executed his influence on the less reputable population of sixteenth-century London.

CHAPTER NINE

End of an Epoch

Between Kew Gardens and the southward curve of the river lies an open space containing a golf-course, an observatory and various sports and recreation grounds, and still bearing the name of the Old Deer Park, and at its southern end, fronting on to Richmond Green, may be seen a gateway of brick, practically all that remains of the straggling Renaissance palace in which, in March 1603, the old Queen died. She was nearly seventy years of age, she had been Queen of England for more than forty years and had ruled it single-handed, as no woman has done before or since. Time and again her subjects and counsellors had urged her to marry, time and again she had put them off with witty, kindly words, and more than once had declared her intention to live and die a maiden queen. To grant her people's request would offer only two alternatives—marriage with a foreign prince, or with one of her own subjects. Her sister, Mary of England, had done the one, her cousin, Mary of Scotland, had done the other, and for each of them the act had meant bitter personal unhappiness and—what counted for more with Elizabeth—trouble, bloodshed and rebellion in the land she ruled. That, at all costs, the Queen was determined to avoid. For the technical work of government she relied upon her ministers, but they were ministers of her own choosing, and she kept a shrewd watch on all they did, never fearing to call them sharply to account if she thought they took too much upon themselves. Now she had outlived them all: Cecil who had served her sister before her, and whom she had picked out, on her own accession, as a man 'not to be corrupted by any manner of gift'; Walsingham, who had worn himself out in the task of establishing an intelligence service not to be surpassed for generations; the courtiers who had flattered her, like Robert Dudley, who had so nearly won her heart, and that other Robert, the Earl of Essex, whom she had sent to the block for treason, though she broke her own heart in the doing of it. Two men were left from the 'old guard', and neither of them had been at her side, like Cecil and Walsingham, in the task of government. Her kinsman the Earl of Nottingham had commanded her fleet against the Armada, and now was Lord High Admiral, nearly as old as she; while Walter Ralegh, once a fascinating and ambitious young man with bold manners and a strong West Country accent, was ageing in his turn, though he still had many years of frustration and captivity to endure before a suspended sentence would be put into execution and the last of the Elizabethans meet his death under the axe in Old Palace Yard. Her 'next heir of blood and descent' was the King of Scotland, great-grandson of her father's elder sister, but the direct line of the Tudors was coming to an end. She was old, and she was dying, and she was the last.

Too weak to sit on her throne, she still refused to go to bed, but lay huddled on cushions on the floor. The coronation ring had been filed from her finger, because its hoop was fretting its way into her very flesh. Robert Cecil, the son of her famous and incorruptible servant, was anxiously at her elbow, waiting and pestering her for some hint of what was to happen next, and urging her to take to her bed. An ill-judged expression from him struck from her a momentary flash of the old fire, and the withering retort: '*Must*? That is no word to use to princes!' Finally, when all else was unavailing, they sent to Arundel House for the Earl of Nottingham, her cousin and her oldest surviving friend. He came to her, fresh from the death and burial of his wife, and by his persuasion she was induced to let her attendants put her to bed.

The last sight of her, recorded by Sir Robert Carey, suggests that she had suffered a slight stroke, with its accompanying speechlessness and partial paralysis, for she lay on her back with one hand outside the bedclothes, and this and her eyes, it seems, were all that moved. She had put her hand to her head when they asked if she would have the King of Scots to succeed her; now John Whitgift, the aged Archbishop of Canterbury, was kneeling at her side, examining her upon her faith, and hand and eyes were moving again in answer to his questions. 'Then', says Carey, 'the good man told her plainly what she was, and what she was to come to, and though she had been long a great Queen here upon earth, yet shortly she was to yield an account of her stewardship to the King

103

of kings'. He continued in prayer till for very weariness he tried to rise from his knees and take his leave, but the hand on the bed moved in a helpless signal, and he went on in prayer for a long half-hour. Again he tried to rise, again the hand stirred to restrain him, and he prayed for half an hour more. Then it was late, and it would seem she must have been asleep, for Carey and the Archbishop were able to withdraw, as did all save the Queen's personal attendants, and very soon afterwards, in the early hours of the morning, word was brought to Carey that Elizabeth was dead. No one knows exactly what was the token that he took with him when he rode to Edinburgh with the news, or what had been arranged beforehand in the matter of passwords, for he had gone off without the consent of the Council, but there is reason to believe that he carried the sapphire ring that had been so lately filed from its owner's hand. Carey's own narrative merely relates that he told King James that he had brought him 'a blue ring from a fair lady', and that the King took it and looked upon it and said: 'It is enough. I know by this you are a true messenger.'

New brooms, it is well known, sweep clean. The new King saw no reason to wear, or even to suggest, mourning for his predecessor. The black, white, or black-and-white attire that had been the regular wear at Elizabeth's court gave place to light colours such as red and yellow, and when the Marquis de Rosny paid a ceremonial visit of condolence, as representative of his master, Henri IV of France, he was somewhat disconcerted to learn that he would cause the greatest displeasure if he were to appear in black, as he had intended. The expensive mourning-suits that he had provided for himself and his suite remained unworn among the luggage, and the delegation, at some severe cost to its leader's sense of propriety, presented itself at Whitehall in the travelling-dress worn on the most ordinary occasions.

And as it was with cloak and doublet, so it was with much of London itself. Progress was to be the order of the day. Elizabeth's timber banqueting-chamber was pulled down and superseded by a permanent building of stone, still to be seen in Whitehall. Inigo Jones, its architect, was in great demand to plan and design new buildings and to add unexpected embellishments to old ones. The burning of the steeple of St Paul's in 1561 had led to the making of various designs for a new spire—one, a colourful elevation in pure Italianate style, is preserved in the library of the Society of Antiquaries—and money was subscribed, by the Queen and others, for the rebuilding, but nothing was done, 'through whose default, God knoweth', as Stow non-committally observes. Now, however, Jones equipped the building with something quite different and even more incongruous, re-facing the west end of the Norman structure with a pillared portico, which must have been impressive in itself but was completely unsuited to the main mass of the cathedral. The great houses of the Strand were arising in new splendour, and he played his part here in turn, as can be seen from the graceful water-gate of York House, now far away from the waterside and surrounded by the greensward of the Embankment Gardens. Farther north, he was employed by Francis Russell, Earl of Bedford, to lay out what we should now call a speculative building-estate on the old convent garden of the Westminster monks. For the first time a patron was commissioning an architect to design, not one house for the patron himself to live in, but a quadrangle of houses, with a church on one side of it, in the certainty that persons of quality would want to live in them, and pay to live in them, as soon as they were built. Covent Garden, and St Paul's Church on the west side of it, have gone through certain vicissitudes, but the observer can easily see the general outline of Inigo Jones's plan. It was new, it was revolutionary, it was all part of an instinctive movement to sweep out the ideas and traditions of Elizabethan London and replace them with something in keeping with the new age that was felt to be beginning.

What the 'improvers' left, the Great Fire took, when it swept through London in those terrible September days of 1666. King Charles II is reported by a contemporary Londoner to have taken an active personal part in the work of fire-fighting, with his brother the Duke of York, 'handing the water in buckets when they stood up to the ancles in water, and playing the engines for many hours together, as they did at the Temple and Cripplegate'. These are the words of a letter in the London Museum, so we may well owe to Charles, among others, the preservation of the fine Elizabethan structure of Middle Temple Hall. That, and certain portions of Staple Inn, are the only considerable pieces of characteristic Elizabethan architecture that London can still claim to show. The statue of the Queen, high on a wall by the church of St Dunstan-in-the-West in Fleet Street, is said to be the one set up in her own lifetime upon Ludgate, when that gate was rebuilt in 1586, but it has not the look of an Elizabethan figure. Crown, ruff and farthingale are there, to be sure, but the shape and poise of the crown are not Elizabethan in appearance, there is a Lely-like look in the row of small curls across the forehead and the way the hair is puffed out on both sides over the ears, not to mention a suggestion of loose comfort and broken folds about the royal robe itself, which make it very different from the unquestionable, uncompromising effigy that lies on Elizabeth's tomb at Westminster. Crown and sceptre are gone, but the stern old face with its arched brows and narrow lips has more in common with the portraits, coins and character of the Queen than the comparatively vacuous figure that stares out over the traffic of Fleet Street and the Strand. It is more reasonable to assume that the original statue on Ludgate was irreparably damaged in the Fire, and that the present effigy is a replacement, carved in the late seventeenth century and influenced by the artistic traditions of the time.

Fig. 29 *Head from the funeral effigy of Elizabeth I—the wig a restoration* (London Museum)

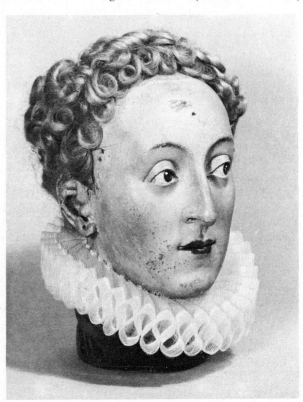

Very different is a carved wooden portrait head now in the London Museum (*Fig. 29*). For more than a hundred years it belonged to a life-size figure of Elizabeth displayed at the Tower, supposedly in the act of reviewing her troops at Tilbury, and first set up there in the latter part of the eighteenth century. Examination of it a few years ago showed that its surface-coat of sallow eighteenth- or nineteenth-century paint covered something infinitely fresher and finer. The outer coat was slowly and skilfully removed, and brought with it an underlying layer of dirt, which had at once concealed and preserved the earlier pigments beneath. The head was taken up to Westminster for comparison with the figure on the tomb and the wooden portrait head of Anne of Denmark, carved and painted some years later by Maximilian Colte and Jan de Critz, who had been the makers of a similar figure carried at the funeral of Elizabeth in 1603. The result was exciting. Sculpturally the wooden head resembled the stone one on the tomb, even to such details as the elaborate configuration of the ears, while the technique of construction and the style of painting corresponded with the head of Anne of Denmark's funeral effigy, still preserved in the Abbey Museum. The piece was established as the head of the wooden figure of Elizabeth that had lain, robed and crowned, upon her coffin when it was carried through the streets to its vault at Westminster, and had been kept afterwards, among other similar effigies, in the purlieus of the Abbey till it got so dirty, dilapidated and disreputable that it was no longer fit to be shown to visitors, and was superseded by the wax figure purchased in 1760 and still exhibited in the Undercroft. No one recorded, and presumably no one cared, what was done with the old effigy, but the head must have been given or sold to someone at the Tower who freshened it up by putting a coat of paint on top of the dirt, dressed it in the upper half of a foot-combat armour that had been made for Henry VIII, and used it as the nucleus of a new portrait-group in the 'Spanish Armoury'.

Somewhat unexpectedly, this interesting fragment appears to suggest something more about the Queen. Under its rather sallow coat of Georgian paint or Victorian repaint, it had the slightly haggard, hollow-cheeked appearance that we have been accustomed to associate with Elizabeth in her latter years. Something of the sort, likewise, can be observed in the stone figure upon the tomb. In the wooden head and the stone effigy the sculptor—probably Maximilian Colte in both instances—has not avoided a certain hollowness about the cheeks and eyes, and a slight line from each nostril to the corner of the mouth. In the monochrome paint, and the uncoloured stone, they cast fine shadows that could not escape notice, but when the head was stripped to its original fresh-coloured complexion, the matter became different indeed. The red upon the cheeks had not been applied at its usual height, where the skin-muscles and small veins are stretched across the cheekbone, but lower down, almost level with the lips, and consequently hiding that hollowness of the cheeks that the sculptor had been conscientious enough to re-produce. The upper eyelids, and the orbits under the overhang of the brow, are very slightly shadowed with green, and the effect of the whole is to conceal the hollows and give the face a fuller, rounder aspect.

To those especially who, like the present writer, knew the head in its almost-monochrome state, the transformation is disconcerting in its completeness, and illuminating in respect of the possibilities that lay in the hands of the Queen's tire-women. What had been achieved on a wooden effigy must have been possible, to some extent at least, on a living face; and the haggard, raddled mask dear to the imagination of Horace Walpole and his imitators must give place to a face that, by careful painting, could still contrive to look reasonably full and young. The portrait-painters of that day need not be dismissed as mere time-servers and flatterers, for this interesting piece of portrait sculpture and painting does a great deal to support the tradition that Elizabeth carried much of her famous beauty to the very threshold of the grave.

CHAPTER TEN

In Search of
the Elizabethans

The seeker after relics of Elizabethan London has a varied task before him, and much will depend upon his personal interests and imaginative power. He may like, in the first instance, to go to Chancery Lane underground station and look up at the characteristic timbering and gables of Staple Inn, imagining what they must have been like when the shops below them had not yet been extended forward, as most of them have been by now, and the overhang of the first floor was sufficient to form a shelter from the rain, or from miscellaneous slops emptied out of upper windows and imperilling the hats, heads and cloaks of the unwary. Holborn was not the busy thoroughfare that it is today, but a broad country road outside the city, just beginning to be built upon, at the London end, but running westwards through open pasture to the church that still bears the name of St Giles's-in-the-Fields. Not far from the station entrance, Fetter Lane turns down towards Fleet Street, and though wartime bombing and subsequent rebuilding have opened out wide vistas here and there, enough of the street-plan is left to show what it must have been like when the shops on each side of it were over-hanging buildings erected after the Staple Inn fashion, with signs, fixed or swinging, that further obscured the sky. The sight of a present-day omnibus negotiating the turn into Fleet Street is sufficiently alarming to suggest the infinite complications that must have existed when the road was no wider than it is now, save that it had no stone pavements for pedestrians, and instead of being cambered, sloped inwards to a central gutter.

In such a place it is easy to imagine the hazards caused by horsemen, singly or in company, by trains of pack-mules laden with bales and boxes, and, towards the end of the reign, by the 'Cars,

Draies, Carts & Coaches' of which Stow complains with such eloquence. At the street-corners one might expect to find low but sturdy stone uprights, not unlike milestones, set firmly in the ground to protect the wooden corner-posts of the houses from being continually jarred, or even broken or displaced, by the wheels of passing traffic. Similar uprights, in such streets as were wide enough to take them, were set at more or less regular intervals on each side to confine horses and pack-animals to the middle of the road and keep them from blocking it utterly from side to side and jostling the very doors, windows and shop-fronts. Many lanes and alleys, where they opened into the larger streets, were fitted with heavy chains, which could be rapidly hooked across the mouth of the lane on any sudden emergency to prevent too easy an inrush of turbulent characters intent on riot and pillage, or in flight from the official keepers of the Queen's Peace. Without some such precaution, the minor scuffles and battles that cropped up periodically among the more quarrelsome and irresponsible apprentices and serving-men would have had too good a chance of spreading into the byways and leading to serious damage, whereas in the broader, lighter streets they could be kept under better control.

Looking to the right from the foot of the lane, one can see the high pedestal of the griffin, where once Temple Bar marked the end of the Liberties, and where now Fleet Street changes its identity and becomes the Strand. Not so far away the church of St Dunstan-in-the-West once more tells the time with its famous clock and bell-beating figures, restored to it after many years of exile in Regent's Park, and next door to them stands that rather Lely-like Elizabeth in her niche, with an inscription commemorating her earlier station upon the façade of Ludgate. Farther down still, the half-timbered buildings on the south side of the Strand illustrate the change that had come over London architecture by the seventeenth century, when the beams were used not only to provide a framework but as a ground for more or less elaborate carving. The decorated woodwork of Stuart architecture has a character of its own, very easily distinguished from the plain house-timbering of the Tudors.

Even more strongly marked is the change from Tudor to Stuart architecture that dominates the view in the other direction. One does not have to go far along Fleet Street in the direction of the City before becoming conscious of a great dome rising between towers, and a hill that sweeps upward to be crowned by the cathedral church that is the masterpiece of Wren. The Italian classical style, practised so intensively by Inigo Jones after Elizabeth's death, has been brought by the later architect to such a pitch of excellence and appropriateness in this building, that it takes a conscious effort to remember that the Elizabethan 'Paul's' was a very different structure, but one with an impressiveness of its own. Look up Ludgate Hill and imagine it surmounted by something like Salisbury Cathedral, with Gothic buttresses and a thin spire apparently reaching as high as Heaven. The substitution does much to alter, in a moment, the whole character of London, revealing it as essentially a medieval city—which, as we have seen, it was.

That is the cathedral to be seen, spire and all, on Hogenberg's map in the *Civitates*, that is the cathedral as Elizabeth knew it when she came to her capital city as a young Queen, but she had not been three years on her throne before the change began. On 4 June 1561 the spire was struck by lightning and burned down to the stonework of the tower and bell-chamber, the roofs of the nave and aisles caught fire from it, and in four hours all the woodwork was burned. The Queen was 'much grieved for the loss of so beautifull a monument', and gave a thousand marks in gold, and a warrant for a thousand cartloads of timber from the royal forests, to head the subscription-list for the rebuilding. The church was given a temporary roof of boards and lead within a month of the disaster, the aisles were completely re-roofed before the end of the year, and the mighty roof-timbers of the nave, choir and transepts were cut and fitted in Yorkshire, brought to London by sea—a quicker and easier passage than could have been achieved over country roads—and set in place and leaded by April 1566, but no new steeple arose over the central tower, and the cathedral was only half the height that it had been. Five hundred and twenty feet above the ground it had held its gilded weathercock as a landmark for all to see; now the central tower rose for two hundred and sixty feet only and ended in a shallow-pitched roof, to remain so for a hundred years, till another and greater fire brought it to an end, with the larger part of the city in which it stood.

In spite of this devastation, however, there are still traces and memorials of great Elizabethans to be seen in the City here and there. Gresham's Royal Exchange is gone, save for the stone pavement that he is said to have brought from Turkey, but his tomb yet remains in the church of St Helen's Bishopsgate. In that same church is the armed effigy of Sir William Pickering, who had served

Henry VIII and all his children as soldier, ambassador and commercial diplomat, and had been considered, in his day, a possible candidate for the hand of the young Elizabeth; while the church of St Andrew Undershaft contains perhaps the most famous tomb and effigy of them all. In the north-east corner is the monument of an old man who sits upright, eternally writing in a book. It is John Stow (*frontispiece*), tailor, antiquary, historian, topographer and finally, in his old age, licensed beggar, by permission of King James I. After a lifetime devoted to his trade and his self-appointed task of seeking and recording the history of England and the antiquities of London, he would appear to have died in poverty, but his widow must have found generous helpers in her bereavement, for the monument—no mean one—is recorded to have been set up at her expense. Stow died, at the age of eighty, on 8 April 1605, and every year, at about that time, a commemorative service is held in the church, a tribute to his memory is spoken from the pulpit, and the Lord Mayor of London places a new quill pen in the hand of the statue. The ceremony is of comparatively recent introduction, but an expressive tribute by one of his contemporaries appears in Howes's edition of Stow's *Annals*, issued in its revised form many years after the old man's death. An account of his life, his work and his personal appearance is given among the biographies of distinguished men at the end of Elizabeth's reign, and the reference to it in the Index is worded: '*Stowe*: This Stowe that made this Chronicle is become a part of the Chronicle himselfe, where see both his life and death, 811, 1, 5'. He could hardly have found a more appropriate epitaph.

On the south side of the Strand is the entrance to the precincts of the Temple. Most of its architecture is typical of the late seventeenth century, and some indeed is later still, including the replacements needed after enemy bombing in the late war, but the Elizabethan beauty of Middle Temple Hall is still to be seen, with its trophies of armour associated with the Earl of Leicester and the elaborate woodwork of its panelling and screens. Going down towards the river, one can turn up-stream along the Embankment and make one's way to Westminster, passing by lawns and gardens where Inigo Jones's water-gate and the far older retaining-wall of Wolsey's palace appear half-buried in the turf; on through Old Palace Yard where Ralegh, last of the great Elizabethans, gave the word of command for his own death to an executioner whose nerve was on the point of failing him; and so to the church of St Margaret, where he lies buried, and the Abbey hard by, where Elizabeth shares a tomb with that unhappy elder sister who so nearly sent her to the scaffold.

Many of the Elizabethan monuments in the Abbey are of special interest to students of costume and armour, for though the principal figures are often half-shrouded in mantles appropriate to their rank, the stone sons and daughters kneeling around the tombs are shown in ordinary dress. More than that, they are particularly valuable because they show us what most of the portraits and the recumbent effigies do not—namely, what they looked like from behind. Young Robert Cecil has already been mentioned, kneeling in doublet, breeches and short cloak at the foot of his mother's tomb in the little chapel of St Nicholas, just south of the stairs going up to that of Henry VII; and in the corresponding chapel on the north side, that of St Paul, is a wealth of military and civilian costume on the tombs of two distinguished lawyers, Sir John Puckering and Sir Thomas Bromley. Puckering held the office of Lord Keeper of the Great Seal, and lies on his tomb in robes and ruff, while one of the two figures high up on the moulding of the monument carries the stiff, square, tasselled bag in which the Seal is traditionally kept, and which is nowadays associated with the office of the Lord Chancellor. Down below, in the foreground, kneel his three sons and five daughters, the sons in little doublets with turn-down collars instead of ruffs, but disconcertingly wearing long skirts like their sisters for, as many family groups remain to show us, Elizabethan small boys were kept in petticoats for some years before they were 'breeched'. The girls wear gowns cut like their mother's, over very small farthingales, and the characteristic 'French hood', with its folded flap of velvet hanging straight down behind and setting off the erect and steady carriage of the head and neck. Sir Thomas Bromley's daughters, on a neighbouring monument, have similar hoods, but loose-bodied gowns without farthingales, and their brothers, being older than the Puckering children, are represented in armour. Sir Thomas himself wears an open gown of rich brocade, with long hanging sleeves reminiscent of the Londoner in the *Civitates* map.

Other legal figures are Sir Thomas Heskett, Attorney of the Court of Wards and Liveries, facing down the north transept, and Judge Owen in a similar attitude in the south aisle, wearing his judicial robes, hood and cap, and looking very much as if he were unsuccessfully trying to get to sleep in a railway-train. There is

113

more repose in the formal figure of William Thynne, a little to the east of him, lying fully armed, save for the helmet and gauntlets, on a long strip of rush matting, with his head resting on the roll of it, but the most elaborate study of armour is that on the tomb of Sir Francis Vere, in the chapel of St John the Evangelist to the north of that of the Confessor. That great soldier was not killed in battle, but died in his bed, and is represented in shirt and mantle according-ly, but four armed men kneel at the corners of the tomb, supporting on their shoulders a slab on which the dead man's armour is laid out as it might be for a kit-inspection, or in readiness to be carried at his funeral. Over his head the stone close-helmet raises its forest of stone plumes; the pauldrons, or shoulder-pieces, lie next to it, showing the intricacy of their rivets and interior straps; the hollow cuirass sits bolt upright in the middle, between the gauntlets and vambraces that protected the arms; and the leg-armour reaches out to the far end of the slab. This treatment of the armour gives a good view of the borders of thick leather that lined most of the pieces to avoid unnecessary scraping or clattering, and the ornamental edging, cut in scallops or 'pickadills', that was all that could be seen of it from the outside.

Elizabethan armour of English make is seen to the best advantage in the Tower of London, which has an unrivalled collection of the work of the armourers first established at Greenwich by Henry VIII and maintained there for more than a hundred years. Costume in general may be studied in the London Museum, which possesses examples not only of the fashionable attire of the courtier, but of the sober black cut-velvet that would pass its wearer practically any-where, and—rarer perhaps than either—a short-sleeved blouse and full, round breeches of the kind worn by the watermen who plied their craft all over London's river, or the sailors who manned the ocean-going ships that lay at anchor in the Pool. In the same collection are specimens of the flat, round cap of knitted and felted wool, characteristic of the London apprentice, the close-fitting coif for the thin-haired skull of an elderly man, and the ear-flapped cap of the old-fashioned merchant, all dug up in Finsbury and preserved by the chemical action of the soil in the marshy area that was called the Moor. Before it was found possible to build upon this ground, the space was used not only for archery, wrestling and military exercises but for the dumping of miscellaneous rubbish, notably old caps, old shoes and clippings of cloth and leather from the tailors' and cobblers' workshops, including quite a number of codpieces, those curious and clumsy appendages of Germanic origin, which adorned the fall-front of Tudor and early Elizabethan hose but went out of fashion in the third quarter of the sixteenth century.

Material dug up in London earth usually appeals to the mind rather than to the eye, but a find that is not only archaeologically interesting but aesthetically attractive is the hoard of late Elizabethan and early Jacobean jewellery that was dug up in Cheapside in 1912 and purchased on the spot for the newly-formed London Museum, though in view of the national importance, artistic interest and City associations of the find, certain pieces from it were later transferred to the British Museum, the Victoria and Albert Museum and the Guildhall Museum. There are rings, buttons, pendants, a pomander, jewelled objects like tiny fan-mounts, to hold plumes of feathers in the brims of hats, yards of fine gold chain, jewelled or enamelled, small toy-like ornaments of precious or semi-precious stone, and a tiny gold watch set in the heart of a great emerald, with a translucent sliver of the stone mounted like a watch-glass on a golden hinge to protect the hands and the dial. A few of the pieces belong to the early seventeenth century, and it is a reasonable conjecture that the treasure was the stock-in-trade of some London jeweller who buried it under the floor of his house in Cheapside when temporarily leaving London in one of the epidemics of plague that are known to have occurred in London in the reign of James I.

Other London Museum exhibits, of interest rather for their associations than their appearance, are an elaborate steelyard made for Sir Thomas Gresham and bearing his name upon the weighted hook and his armorial bearings upon the bracket, the copper plate engraved with part of an otherwise unknown map of Elizabethan London, and the stem and foot of a Venetian glass goblet dug up on the site of Verzelini's factory at Crutched Friars; but there are one or two individual pieces that have a certain degree of elegance, and even beauty. The carved and painted head of the Queen has been mentioned and described already, but another exhibit, of a very different kind, provides an unexpected illustration of her early religious policy.

In September 1533 the Lord Mayor of London, Sir Stephen Peacock, had gone down-stream in his barge to Greenwich to pay a formal visit of congratulation on the birth of the little Princess Elizabeth. Three years later he had bequeathed to the church of St Martin, Ludgate, a silver-gilt monstrance for the displaying of the Sacred Host. More than twenty years after that, when Elizabeth became Queen, the Reformed faith was in the ascendant and the churches of London had to amend their plate accordingly. A royal proclamation laid down that pre-Reformation chalices were to have their bowls altered to the beaker-shaped form that was now the only lawful one for the communion cup, and bishops all over the country were enjoined to make sure, in their Visitations, that this had been done. This simple substitution made it far less easy for the forbidden Mass to be celebrated in secret, since there was no longer available a vessel consecrated to the rite of the older church, and consequently less opportunity, and less temptation, for an accommodating incumbent to use his church and his plate for either service alternatively as required. It appears, however, that it was not only chalices that were thus altered, for a large communion-cup in the museum has a bowl of the orthodox Reformed pattern and the hallmark for 1559, surmounting a stem and foot of almost Gothic outline, with an inscription enjoining the reader to pray for the soul of Stephen Peacock and Margaret his wife, 'which gave this in worship of the Sacrament'. Sir Stephen's monstrance, like so many other pieces in London and out of it, has conformed to the regulations of the newer church, and of the new Queen who declared herself its Supreme Governor.

The London Museum devotes itself to the illustration of London's history, but the Victoria and Albert Museum was founded to preserve and exhibit samples of the applied arts. It is to this institution, therefore, that we turn for splendid examples of the craftsmanship of all countries, classified primarily according to material. The Department of Metalwork shows us the finest examples of plate in precious metals or alloy, jewellery—including Drake's Armada Jewel, already mentioned—and a certain amount of armour; for furniture we turn naturally to the Department of Woodwork, and for glass and pottery to that of Ceramics. In all these Departments the scope is not confined to London alone, as heretofore; fine examples from the Continent and the East are also to be seen there, showing how the craftsmen of other countries approached their various problems, and how far these, and their aims and designs, corresponded or contrasted with our own. The Department of Textiles concentrates largely on the various fabrics and their treatment. Though it in its turn shows costumes, these belong rather to the later periods, and the general emphasis has lain on the techniques of their making and design rather than the appearance of those who wore them. Here, accordingly, is the place in which to look for the finest examples of that embroidery in coloured silks for which Elizabethan ladies were so widely renowned, as well as 'black-work' of the kind illustrated in the London Museum dress. Certain portions of Sir Paul Pindar's house, which formerly stood in Bishopsgate, are preserved here, and serve again to show, by the Jacobean elaboration of their ornament and the very fineness of their techniques, be it of carved beam or plaster ceiling, the change that was coming over domestic architecture in the years after Elizabeth's death.

The City proper, its relics and its institutions, form the province of the Guildhall Museum, justly famous for its Roman collection and for its examples of London architectural features of many periods, particularly that which immediately succeeded the devastation of the Great Fire. Its relics of the Elizabethan city are archaeologically valuable although, consisting as they do for the most part of excavated material, they are largely fragmentary and not always immediately impressive to the beholder. An exception to this generality, however, must be made at once, in favour of the magnificent collection of early gloves, mostly of seventeenth-century date but including certain Elizabethan examples, and the appropriate section of the material exhibited in this museum by the Museum of Leathercraft.

Oldest and most famous of all these institutions is, of course, the British Museum. Here the scope is so wide that the available display-area, large as it is, remains all too small for the wealth of material that might be shown, and it takes time and concentration to pick out, among so many and such varied treasures, those particularly relevant to Elizabethan London. One comes upon them unexpectedly here and there, when a name on a label brings the sudden realization that here is something intimately connected with some figure so familiar from history as almost to have become a legend. Here, for instance, is a letter written by Ralegh to Leicester, when that self-willed and imperious favourite had disgraced himself by going too far, and needed to be reassured in a postscript that matters had now blown over, and that it was safe for him to appear at Court again. Here, too, are letters in the hand of Elizabeth, with her sweeping decorative signature, and here the unique manuscript play of *Sir Thomas More*, certain passages of which are claimed, with considerable justification, to be not only the work, but in the actual handwriting, of Shakespeare. In another gallery a group of yellowing discs of wax, inscribed with impressive and cabalistic signs, were the property of the famous Dr John Dee, mathematician and astrologer, whom the young Queen consulted when selecting an auspicious date for her coronation. The small ones apparently served as insulators, under the feet of his table, and their larger companion, in the middle of it, supported his crystal or 'magic mirror of cannel coal'—really a disc of obsidian, now housed in the same collection—the pentacles and planetary symbols being supposed to guard the apparatus against disturbing influences from the earth.

Looking at such objects, and realizing who must have seen and handled them in former days, one feels a sudden sense of nearness to those great figures of the past, particularly to the pale, hard, lonely woman who was the greatest of them all. Unlike most royal figures, before her time and after, she was of native stock on both sides, and delighted in her claim to be 'mere English'. On one hand she was descended from Kings of England, on the other from a Lord Mayor of London. In her veins ran the blood of both the cities, and in Guildhall and Leadenhall, no less than in Whitehall, she could command the allegiance of subjects who felt not only deference to their anointed sovereign but admiration and affection for someone whom they proudly regarded as one of themselves. London and Elizabeth belonged to each other in an almost literal sense: they appreciated each other, understood each other, and each would appear, periodically, in splendid array in the other's honour or for the other's pleasure. We have seen how the whole character of the city underwent a change in the course of the Queen's long reign, but she herself remained true to her own motto *Semper Eadem*, ever the same through all alteration. Her dominating personality had made the very changes appear less weighty and significant; and her death, when it came to her in the middle of her seventieth year, meant the breaking of the last link between the new London and the old.

Index

FYNNESBVRIE FIELD.

Fynnesb Courte.

Dogg hows.

MOOR FIELD.

S.Thophins

MOOR GATE.